CHRIST AND THE SAILOR

Other books by Peter F. Anson

" I will make you into fishers of men " [*Matthew 4.19*]
One of the maritime fraternity of the *Petits Frères de Jésus*,
working as deckhand on a Breton deep-sea trawler

CHRIST AND THE SAILOR

*A study of the maritime incidents
in the New Testament*

BY
PETER F. ANSON

With a Foreword by the Most Rev.
THOMAS D. ROBERTS, S.J.
Formerly Archbishop of Bombay

LONDON
BURNS & OATES

NIHIL OBSTAT: CAROLVS DAVIS, S.T.L.
CENSOR DEPVTATVS
IMPRIMATVR: E. MORROGH BERNARD
VICARIVS GENERALIS
WESTMONASTERII: DIE XV MARTII MCMLIV

MADE AND PRINTED IN GREAT BRITAIN AT
THE CHAPEL RIVER PRESS, ANDOVER, HANTS,
FOR BURNS OATES AND WASHBOURNE, LTD.,
28, ASHLEY PLACE, LONDON, S.W.1

First published 1954

TO THE PRIESTS AND SEMINARISTS OF *LA MISSION DE LA MER*, THE MARITIME FRATERNITY OF THE *PETITS FRÈRES DE JÉSUS*, AND THE MEMBERS OF *LA JEUNESSE MARITIME CHRÉTIENNE*, IN MEMORY OF THREE MONTHS IN FRANCE, JUNE–AUGUST, 1951

FOREWORD

Much time spent among sailors, especially in Bombay during the war years, that brought every type of ship there, convinced me that the Church has paid but a small part of the debt she owes to them.

As the Cardinal Archbishop of Westminster has said in his preface to Mr. Anson's *The Church and the Sailor*, " he is undoubtedly the greatest living authority on the Sea Apostolate past and present. No one, then, is better qualified to tell the story of the Church and the Sailor." In that book he shows how far we have fallen short in the past, the good work of the present time, how we may prepare for a brighter future.

In this new book, *Christ and the Sailor*, is an appeal to all of us, based on the lofty motive of our Lord's special love for those he foresaw as destined, in the nature of their calling, to become neglected. St. John, who knew best the Heart on which he rested, never hesitated to apply to himself the most startling of titles, " That disciple whom Jesus loved ". In fact our Saviour's predilection for one individual was extended to that man's profession. His best-beloved interpreter and the chief of the whole band were but two called from the waters to be his " Fishers of Men ".

May they obtain for the author his best reward in the sharing by very many of his conviction that we must all help and be helped by the sailor, prime favourite of our Lord.

✠ T. D. ROBERTS, S.J.,

Formerly Archbishop of Bombay.

vii

ACKNOWLEDGMENTS

My thanks are due to the following for their advice and criticism: the Rev. J. M. Butel, S.J. (Executive Secretary, International Council, *Apostolatus Maris*); the Rev. R. More O'Ferrall (Secretary of the English and Welsh National Board of the Apostleship of the Sea); the Rev. Desmond Chute; the Rev. Fr. M. Begouen-Demeaux, O.P.; the Rev. R. H. Redfern (Literary Secretary, Missions to Seamen); Mr. Frank G. G. Carr (Director of the National Maritime Museum, Greenwich); Mr. Alex. J. McKay; Mr. John D. Smith; Mr. George Smith; also to the Librarian of St. Benedict's Abbey, Fort Augustus, for the loan of reference books.

I must also thank Messrs. Burns Oates and Washbourne for permission to quote from Mgr. Knox's translation of the New Testament.

P.F.A.

CONTENTS

APPENDICES

LIST OF ILLUSTRATIONS

[1] Photographs by Shepherd & Ritchie, Macduff.
[2] Photographs by George W. F. Ellis, London.
[3] Photograph by H. Jenkins, Lowestoft.

INTRODUCTION

WE are so accustomed to pictures and statues of SS. Peter, Andrew, James and John, clothed in flowing draperies, with haloes round their heads, that it is easy to forget that these four Apostles spent their youth and early manhood in catching and selling fish. In the great basilica at Rome, erected over the tomb of Peter the Fisherman, there is little or nothing to remind us of his job, except the mosaic above the central door of the portico or vestibule, depicting him walking on the sea. But few visitors ever notice this mosaic because it is so high up. The famous bronze statue of the Prince of the Apostles in the same basilica, emphasizes his office as Head of the Church and makes no attempt to be the portrait of a working-man. It is even more difficult to remember that Peter was a fisherman when, on some great festival, this statue is vested in a cope of gold brocade and a triple tiara rests on that curly head, the hair of which was often blown about by the breeze or soaked with spray.

It is very seldom that the other three fishermen-Apostles—Andrew, James and John—are depicted in relation to their trade. One of the reasons for writing this book is to strip St. Peter of his cope and tiara, take away his keys, and give him back his nets, lines and boat. I want my readers to forget, for the moment, that Peter was the Prince of the Apostles and to think of him as a fisherman. I wish to stress the fact, so often forgotten, that our Lord's first four disciples and those whom he chose to be his most intimate friends, were *working-men*, who had more knowledge of the fishing industry, fishing gear, boats and the moods of the wind and the waves, than of the Mosaic Law.

If our Lord had to choose an artisan to be the rock upon which his Church was to be built, why did he not select a mason or a carpenter—two trades more closely associated with building? An even more logical choice might have been an experienced clerk-of-the-works to carry out the designs of " Christ the Architect ". Again, if you think of it, Matthew, the tax-collector, was more accustomed to looking after keys than any inshore fisherman. Did it ever occur to Judas, who acted as honorary-treasurer of the apostolic community, that he ought to have been entrusted with the keys of the kingdom of heaven? Why did this Rabbi, as he was known to the people, not call any priests, scribes or elders to be his Apostles? Why did he pass over the rulers and lesser officials of the synagogues? For these men were trained to preach, teach and conduct public worship. The Pharisees and Sadducees, from their point of view, had good reason to be suspicious of the carpenter-evangelist from Nazareth who claimed to be the promised Messias.

When, at last the people of Nazareth drove Jesus out of the town as a dangerous agitator, why did this Carpenter's Son take lodgings with a fisher family in one of the small ports on the Sea of Galilee? Until our Lord went up to Jerusalem for the last time, to face his Passion and Crucifixion, the only " home " he had in this world was with that fisher family in Capharnaum.

There must have been many young men among the followers of John the Baptist who might have been ready to leave him and follow an even greater Preacher, had the call come to them. But it was the fishermen brothers, Andrew and Simon, who received this call. Our Lord understood that men who are accustomed to sailing boats and catching fish—a job that involves a ceaseless watch on the mysterious changes of the weather—acquire a certain outlook on life and particular qualifications seldom found among men who earn their living on land. Having chosen his first four disciples from a maritime community, he shared their life and work to a large extent; in fact, he became one of them.

Here is a point to be stressed: fisher folk are much the same all the world over: the background, even the details of their lives, change very little throughout the ages, just because their trade is mainly controlled by the timeless forces of nature instead of by constantly altered man-made laws. Moreover, this trade produces a particular mentality. No matter what they did or where they went after they had abandoned their boats and their fishing gear, Peter, Andrew, James and John would have gone on forming opinions, making decisions and behaving in emergencies *as fishermen and seafarers*. Their characters would have been moulded before they left all things to follow Christ. You do not instantly change the temperament of a seaman or fisherman by finding him a job ashore. All sorts of little idiosyncrasies and propensities will suddenly assert themselves, the inevitable product of heredity and environment.

Having lived in fairly close contact with all classes of seafarers most of my life, and in the midst of fisher folk for nearly a quarter of a century, I have come to the conclusion that the best way to understand the maritime incidents recorded in the New Testament is to visualize them in terms of contemporary life. This is the reason I have chosen photographs of different aspects of maritime life to-day to illustrate this book, even if it deals with events which took place more than nineteen hundred years ago.

Watch fishermen as they are mending their nets, repairing their gear or painting their boats. Go to sea with them, as Jesus did on the Sea of Galilee, in calm weather and on stormy days and nights. Listen to their conversation, probably much the same subjects as were discussed by Peter, Andrew, James and John —where they have located shoals of fish, how such-and-such a boat got her nets torn, how another was poaching, the amount of fish landed and the prices obtained at the market. It is probable that the fishermen of Bethsaida and Capharnaum had much the same bother about transport for their dried fish to Jerusalem as the fishermen of Britain have when sending their fish to the larger towns and cities. One suspects that the Galilean fishermen used to curse the Roman government for tiresome rules and regulations!

On a hot day, when the sun is shining, one smells the same smells that Jesus must have been conscious of as he wandered along the shore, or sat in any of the boats. There would have been much the same sounds—the lapping of water, the creaking of sails being hoisted, the splash of oars, and the shouts of men. Most likely there was the monotonous chant of the fish-salesman as he marketed the catch from the boats, laid out on the shore. Handle the slithery fish, learn to gut them, and one understands better how the fishermen-Apostles regarded the souls of men in after years. The environment in which our Lord spent much of the three years of his active ministry can be visualized and felt in almost any fishing port to-day.

If one has had the same experience oneself, it is easier to grasp what the Apostles felt when they hauled in their nets full of fish after they had been toiling all night and caught nothing. Only when one has sailed in an open boat in a stiff breeze and wondered if she is going to heel over, can one fully share in the fear and dread of the disciples before our Lord stilled the fury of the wind and the waves. If one has ever been to sea on a wild night and a gale raging, watching the waves breaking over the gunwale or bulwarks, one can understand what was the terror of that Galilean crew when they beheld a man walking towards them over the rise and fall of the waters.

To enter into the spirit of the voyages of the Apostles it is not enough to delve into nautical history or study the topography of the Eastern Mediterranean. The " background " of those voyages is to be found more realistically in any coasting vessel, no matter if she now depends on steam or motor instead of sail. Like the modern tramp-steamer, the sailing ships in which St. Paul and the other Apostles voyaged through the islands of the Aegean and along the coasts of Asia Minor and Syria, put into ports, large and small, to discharge or take on cargoes. When the Christian missionaries went ashore, the " sailor town " in which they found themselves was probably much the same sort of world as it is in any world-port to-day.

In a previous book, entitled *The Church and the Sailor*, I ventured to draw attention to the fact that the Christian apostolate began as a mission to fisher-men. I pointed out that no writer, so far as I could

B

discover, had ever made a thorough investigation of the apostolic action of the Church among seafarers. In that small volume all I could do was to give a rough sketch of how Christ has been revealed to seafarers in the past nineteen hundred years. The need for another book, to serve as an introduction to *The Church and the Sailor*, was obvious. Like its companion this one makes no claim to be exhaustive. Being a marine artist by profession I am fully aware that it would have been wiser to have waited for a Biblical scholar to have tackled the job. I hope and pray that it may be of some use to priests and layfolk whose lives are dedicated to the sea apostolate, especially those who, unlike Peter, Andrew, James and John, have not had the advantage of catching fish at sea before they are sent to catch men.

Low Shore,   PETER F. ANSON.
    Macduff,   *February*, 1954.
      Banffshire.

CHAPTER I

THE JEWS AND THE SEA

Chapter I

THE JEWS AND THE SEA

And the spirit of God moved over the waters—Genesis 1.2.

I will set thy bounds from the Red Sea to the sea of the Philistines—Exodus 23.31.

Thy way is in the sea, and thy paths in many waters—Psalm 76.20.

Sing ye to the Lord . . . you that go down to the sea—Isaias 42.10.

Year in, year out the winds and the waves beat on the long coastline of Palestine. It is an unfriendly coast; an almost unbroken line of sand dunes or low cliffs. There are no bays or promontories, hardly any natural harbours. Even the few creeks and estuaries of small rivers are blocked with mud. This shore " seems as if the land were everywhere saying to the sea: ' I do not wish you, I do not need you! ' And this echoes through most of the Old Testament ".[1]

Israel never took the sea for a friend. The Jews regarded the sea as an enemy. " With no harbour, nor any visible island to tempt Israel to adventure, and no sailor blood in her veins, she hated and feared the sea, and thought of it with ill will. There is little of the wistfulness of romance in her thought of the dwellers in its uttermost parts; little of the sense of beauty in her poetry of the breaking waves. She views the Phoenician trader who does business on the

[1] George Adam Smith, *Historical Geography of the Holy Land*, p. 131.

3

ocean as a person to be astonished at rather than to
be accounted heroic. She exults in the fact that God
has his paths in the great waters, but has no wish to
make any journey there herself. Her angels plant their
feet upon the sea, and she looks forward almost
triumphantly when it will be dried up and disappear.
Meanwhile its inaccessible huge depth is for her poets
a sort of Gehenna—a fit place for throwing off evil
things beyond the chance of their reappearing; sins
are to be cast into it, and offenders with millstones on
their necks."[1]

Yet paradoxically enough the religious and social
life of the Jews was bound up with the annual com-
memoration of an outstanding event in their history
directly connected with the sea. " The spray of the
Red Sea is found, as it were, on the inmost hills of
Palestine; and from them it has been wafted throughout the world."[2] For the Passover was a yearly
reminder that the way of God is in the sea and his
path in the great waters.

A whiff of this same salt spray off the Red Sea
comes to us every year at Easter—the Christian
Passover—very faint, perhaps, yet it is there in the
background. The rhythm of the Alleluias seems to
echo the far off murmur of the waves which rolled
back as the clouds poured out their water, and the
earth shook and trembled. The Red Sea " must
have always brought to the mind of those who stood
on its shores, that they were on the waters of a new,
and almost unknown world. Those tides come rolling
in from the vast Indian Ocean; and with the Indian
Ocean the two gulfs (at the northern end of the Red

[1] J. Kelman, *The Holy Land*, p. 23.
[2] Arthur Penrhyn Stanley, *Sinai and Palestine*, p. 34.

Sea) are the chief channels of communication from the Northern world. The white shells which strew their shores, the forests of sub-marine vegetation, which gave the whole sea its Hebrew appellation of the ' Sea of Weeds ', the trees of coral, whose huge trunks may be seen even on the dry shore, with the red rocks and red sand, which especially in the Gulf of Akaba bound its sides—all bring before us the mightier mass of the Red or Erythrean Ocean, the coral strands of the Indian Archipelago, of which these two gulfs with their peculiar products are the northern offshoots."[1]

It was this Red Sea which, for thousands of years to come, formed the basis of the religious imagery of Israel, and thence penetrated into the Christian Church and to all nations of the world. Having passed through the sea, the children of Israel turned their backs on the ocean for ever more. They thought of it as " a stiff stormy line, down the whole length of which there was nothing to tempt men in, so nothing to tempt them out ".[2] The roar and surge on the shore filled the Jews with terror. They felt safer among their mountains and valleys. There was only a vague consciousness of the world beyond that far horizon to the west. The Hebrew word applied to all large pieces of water means ' the west ', and is even used of countries beyond the sea. Hardly anywhere in the Old Testament is the sea mentioned except for symbolical purposes, one of the few exceptions being when Jonas used the sea as a means of escape from God.

There is invariable contrast between the security of the kindly earth and the vast restless ocean. The

[1] Stanley, *op. cit.*, p. 5.
[2] Smith, *op. cit.*, p. 134.

Psalmist wonders at the sea—from afar. " He pictures it as a marvellous creation of God, in which live Leviathan and vast numbers of creeping things— apparently, he peopled it with whales and shell fish. The ships, too, are a wonder, which he admires from a safe distance."[1]   Even the more intimate references to ships and sailors in Psalm 106 are concerned with thanksgiving for rescue from the perils of the deep. They merely arouse a sense of fear.   There is no love for the sea in them.

The Hebrew fear and hatred of the sea was also bound up with religion and patriotism.   The southern parts of the coastal plain of Palestine were inhabited by the Philistines, who were strangers from beyond the ocean, worshipping Dagon the fish-god and Derceto the fish-goddess.   To the north were the even more dangerous Phoenicians, who dwelt on the sea-board of Tyre and Sidon; a race of sea-traders and adventurers, who also worshipped strange gods, and traded in the persons of men.   Having practically no ships of their own until shortly before the Roman conquest of Palestine, the Jews were forced to make use of the services of the rich and powerful Phoenicians for their sea-borne commerce.   Solomon paid the Tyrians to float cedar logs from Lebanon down the coast for building the temple at Jerusalem.

After the return of the Jews from exile in Babylon, their dread of the sea and of ships seems to have increased.   They could not forget having been forced to work as galley slaves in the vessels on the Euphrates, where they laboured at the oars, hoisted sails and hauled on the tackle.[2]   Nevertheless the prophet Isaias

[1] J. Holland Rose, *Man and the Sea*, p. 39.
[2] Cf. Isaias 33.21–23.

shows a wider interest in the sea than most of his predecessors. He writes of the heart of Israel growing " large with the sparkle of the sea; for there is turned upon thee the sea's flood tide, and the wealth of the nations is coming unto thee. . . . Surely towards me the isles are stretching, and ships of Tarshish in the van to bring thy sons from afar ".[1] But Isaias was not thinking of ships manned by Jews, and the ports at which the ships from Spain and the Grecian Isles called were those of Tyre and Sidon.

It was not until about 142 B.C. that the Jews came into the possession of a harbour, when Simon Maccabeus captured Joppa.[2] The first thing to be done was to purge this port of its pagan superstitions and to fill it with " such men as would keep the law ". What actually happened was that, in their zeal for religion, the conquerors drove away most of the merchants and mariners, who wanted to go on worshipping their own sea-gods. In 63 B.C. Pompey annexed Joppa to the Roman province of Syria. Fifteen years later Julius Caesar handed it back to the Jews. When Herod the Great built his great harbour about halfway between Joppa and Mount Carmel in 25 B.C., he named it Caesarea, and Joppa began to decline.

" In Herod the ancient Oriental dread of the sea had no existence. He had himself been across the Mediterranean to Rome, and on his alliance with Rome his own power depended; and when, after his death, his kingdom became a Roman province, the city which he had called by the name of his Imperial patron, was still continued as the seat of

[1] Revised Version, 60.8–9.
[2] 1 Mach. 14.5.

the Roman governor, for the same reason as that which induced him to select the site—its maritime situation. From that sea-girt city, Pontius Pilate came yearly across the plain of Sharon, and up the hills, to keep guard on the Festivals at Jerusalem. In the theatre, built by his father—looking out, doubtless, after the manner of all Greek theatres, over the wide expanse of sea, Herod Agrippa was struck with his mortal disease."[1]

Seafaring was a profession which was barred to any orthodox Jew. It was practically impossible for any devout Hebrew to become a sailor, even if he felt the call of the sea. It involved defiling himself with contact with the Gentiles. Except for the very few trading ships at Joppa in the last century before Christ, it would seem that it was only on the Sea of Galilee that Jews were directly earning their living in ships and boats. As our Lord had decided to call his first Apostles from Jews who went down to the sea in ships and did business in great waters. He had no alternative but to look for them among the fishermen of Galilee. He could not have found them on the sea-coast of the Mediterranean.

[1] Stanley, *op. cit.*, p. 262.

CHAPTER II

THE SEA OF GALILEE:
ITS FISHERIES AND FISHERMEN

Chapter II

THE SEA OF GALILEE:
ITS FISHERIES AND FISHERMEN

As he passed along the sea of Galilee, he saw Simon and Simon's brother Andrew casting a net into the sea (for they were fishermen). Jesus said to them, Come and follow me; I will make you into fishers of men—Mark 1.16, 17.

And he went on board one of the boats, which belonged to Simon, and asked him to stand off a little from the land; and, so, sitting down, he began to teach the multitudes from the boat—Luke 5.3.

I. THE SEA OF GALILEE

PERHAPS a first glimpse of the Sea of Galilee has never been more vividly recorded than by Dean Stanley. He says: " Few can fail to have been struck by the sudden flash, as from a rent in the bowels of the earth, when the view of the lake rises from below, and greets the traveller on his downward journey (from Nazareth). . . . In the clearness of the eastern atmosphere, it looks much smaller than it is. From no point on the west side can it be seen completely from end to end; the promontory under which Tiberias stands, cutting off the southern, and the promontory over the plain of Genesareth, the northern extremity, so that the form which it presents is generally that of an oval."[1] The same writer goes on to describe the shores; roughly strewn with black and white stones of volcanic origin, smooth sand, or a texture of shells and pebbles, so minute as

[1] *Sinai and Palestine*, p. 370.

to resemble sand.   Along the shores, here and there
are pink-flowered oleanders.   Shrubs and thorn bushes
are more frequent.   " On this beach, which can be
discerned running like a white line all round the
lake, the hills plant their dark base, descending
nowhere precipitously, but almost everywhere pre-
senting an alternation of soft grassy slopes and rocky
cliffs, occasionally broken away so as to exhibit the
red and grey colours so familiar in the limestone of
Greece."[1]

Another writer has compared the Lake of Genesareth
to " a great flesh-coloured cup, full of blue liquor,
with no translucency, but an aggressive opaqueness,
in sea and shore alike.   The dry atmosphere shows
everything in the sharpest outline, clear-cut and
broken-edged ".[2]   This is how H. V. Morton pictures
the first glimpse of the Lake from the usual approach
from Cana: " Suddenly you see, lying a thousand feet
below, a strip of bright blue.   It is your first sight of
the Sea of Galilee.   As you sometimes look upward
in a mountain gorge and see a strip of blue sky shining,
so in this place you look downward through a gorge
to a distant strip of water as blue as any sky."[3]

The Sea of Galilee, otherwise known as the Lake
of Tiberias, or of Genesareth, measures about 14 miles
from north to south and has an extreme width of
7 miles.   In shape it is an irregular oval.   The water
surface covers approximately 112 square miles.   The
Lake is situated 682 feet below the level of the
Mediterranean.   The depth varies from 25 fathoms

[1] *Sinai and Palestine*, p. 372.
[2] Kelman, *The Holy Land*, p. 247.
[3] *In the Steps of the Master*, p. 180.

towards the north, to 140 fathoms in certain places at
the south, where the Jordan continues its rapid course
down to the Dead Sea. The water is fresh and
drinkable at all seasons. Many streams flow into the
Lake to the north and west, also hot springs, but the
main water supply is the Jordan, which has its sources
among the mountains to the north.

High mountains, rising to over 2,000 feet, enclose
the Lake on every side. To the east they descend
almost to the edge of the water and are very steep in
most places. On the west side the ground rises more
gradually, and the mountains are broken with ravines
and gorges. At the north west the hills fall back,
forming a great natural amphitheatre, known as the
Plain of Genesareth, described in the Talmud as
" The Paradise of the Earth ". Beyond this the soil is
volcanic and the hills slope down gently to the shore.

In the time of Christ the lower slopes were well
wooded. " Where there are now no trees, there were
great woods; where there are marshes, there were noble
gardens; where there is but a boat or two, there were
fleets of sails; where there is one town, there were
many."[1] It is difficult to visualize the same scene
two thousand years ago. " You are driven back upon
the extraordinary present—petrified, uncanny, spectral
—a part of the earth on which some spell has fallen,
and over which some ghastly influence broods, silencing
the daylight and whispering in the darkness."[2]

An almost unbroken line of houses ringed the west
and north shores of the Lake. The towns of Tericheae,
Tiberias, Magdala, Capharnaum, Corozain and Bethsaida, each had from 1,000 to 15,000 inhabitants.

[1] G. A. Smith, *op. cit.*, p. 445.
[2] Kelman, *op. cit.*, p. 249.

To-day all that is left of most of them are broken and tumbled columns and capitals, remains of walls and aqueducts, and other ruins.

2. THE CLIMATE

What the stranger notices at once is the heavy, sultry, enervating climate of this deep basin far below sea-level—a complete contrast to the bracing uplands of Galilee. The marvel is that thousands of people could work and did work here in the past.

In this almost tropical heat, where frosts are practically unknown, even in mid-winter, everything grows abundantly. But the region is notorious for its sudden storms—as violent as was the character of the typical Galilean at the time of Christ. Cold currents of air are sucked down by the narrow gorges. From the distant snow-tipped peak of Hermon, the wind strikes the Lake. In a minute or two the unwrinkled surface of the glass-like water is changed to a rumpled, curling rise and fall of short waves.

The fishermen can foretell such storms almost instinctively. They will refuse to put to sea when all seems set fair. Our Lord hints at such weather-knowledge among the Galilean fishermen of his own time. " When the evening comes, you say, it is fair weather, the sky is red; or at sunrise, there will be a storm to-day, the sky is red and lowering. You know, then, how to read the face of heaven; can you not read the signs of appointed times? "[1]

3. FISHING

Fishing has been carried on from time immemorial. The Lake abounds in fish of many varieties. H. B.

[1] Matthew 16.2–4.

Tristram mentions that he obtained fourteen species, but imagines that there must be at least three times as many. He states that those he caught were the same fish as are found in the Nile: hence a belief among the people that the Sea of Galilee is somehow connected with that river, especially because the sheat-fish is found in both waters. " The density of the shoals can scarcely be conceived by those who have not witnessed them. They frequently cover more than an acre. The fish slowly move in masses— so crowded that the back fins appear on the level of the water. These shoals resemble a violent shower of rain peltering on the surface."[1]

The most common species are the *chromis nilotica* (bream or hasselquist); *clarias macracanthus* (sheat-fish); *labeo barbus canis* (dog-fish); also perch, carp and coracine. The sheat-fish resemble large eels.

According to the Law of Moses,[2] fish were divided into clean and unclean. Only those with scales and fins could be eaten. Fish was an important article of diet among the Jews. It was eaten fresh, dried and pickled.[3] As there was no means of keeping fish fresh in that hot climate, it could be eaten fresh only a short while after it was landed. Hence the development of the fish curing industry. It was sold salted or sun-dried. Sauces were made from fish. The roes of some species were preserved, and regarded as a great delicacy, just as is caviare to-day. Some of the smaller species were cured in much the same way as sardines. The Rabbis were gourmets as regards fish. They compiled cookery books, giving directions on

[1] Tristram, *Natural History of the Bible*, 9th ed., p. 285.
[2] Leviticus 11.9–12.
[3] See pp. 16, 62.

C

the preparation of different species, how to wash and cook them, and how to serve them at table.

The Jerusalem market was mainly supplied from Joppa, but large quantities of preserved fish were taken to the city from Galilee.   One of the north-west gates of Jerusalem was known as the " Fish Gate ", for hard by it was the market.[1]   At one time scandal was caused by the merchants from Tyre selling fish on the Sabbath, but this market was stopped.[2]

Large consignments of fish were imported from abroad, especially from Egypt and Spain.   Josephus writes of the vast amount of fish in the Sea of Galilee. Each port had its fishermen, fish-workers, salesmen and buyers.   Thousands of persons were employed in the industry.   Pliny informs us that fish-curing was started on the Lake of Genesareth by the Greeks. The trade must have expanded enormously, for by the time of Christ barrels of cured fish from Galilee were being exported all over the Mediterranean. There was a great demand for fish every spring when the festival of the Passover took place.   The largest curing yards were at Tericheae, which means " pickling places ".   But every town and village had its fishermen and fish curers.

4.   METHODS OF FISHING

The following methods of fishing were used in the time of Christ, just as they are to-day:

1.   *The casting, or hand-net*—mentioned in Matthew 4.18, Mark 1.16, and John 21.

Tristram writes that the casting net is used either by a naked fisherman, wading from the shore, or from

---

[1] 2 Paralipomenon [2 Chron.] 33.14; Nehemias [2 Esdras] 3.3.
[2] Neh. 13.16.

boats.[1] He describes a fisherman's hut of reeds on the shore of the Lake, beside which a net was spread on the beach to dry. " Out of the rushes a stark naked man appeared, who began to prepare the net for a cast. Having folded it neatly, he swam in with it a little way, cast it (with a rapid motion), and returned by a semi-circular course to the shore, where he gently drew it in with a few fishes caught."[2] The same writer tells us that when he visited Palestine about a century ago, all the cast-net fishermen in Galilee were " stark naked, except for a thick woollen skull-cap ". He mentions that ancient Egyptian monuments depict all persons catching fish and waterfowl *with nets*, naked. The custom would thus seem to be ancient and widespread. (Further details are given on p. 96.)

2. *Seine or drag net* (Luke 5.5; Matthew 13.48).

This type of net, which is let down into deeper water and drawn in by a boat in a semi-circle to the shore, is used to-day as it was by the Apostles. The fishermen work at night, and land their catch at day-break.[3]

3. *Hook* (Matthew 17.27).

Lines are used, with or without rods, by fishermen standing on the shore. Flies are unknown and only bait is put on the hooks.

4. *Harpoon or spear*.

This method is not mentioned in the New Testament, but hinted at in the Book of Job (Authorized Version

[1] *Op. cit.*, p. 289.
[2] *Ibid.*, p. 290.
[3] Further details of the method of working the drag net are given on p. 53.

41.7): " Canst thou fill his skin with barbed irons, or his head with fish spears? " Spearing fish is done at night by torch-light.

5. *Poison.*

Tristram tells us that in his time the fishermen of Galilee were often to be found sitting on the rocks, scattering crumbs poisoned with vitriol over the water. As soon as fish were seen floating on the surface, the men rushed into the sea and collected them.[1]

Fixed nets and weirs were forbidden by the Rabbis long before the time of Christ, mainly for fear of damaging fishing boats on the Lake.[2]

When the fish had been landed it was sorted, for those without scales had to be cast away as unfit for human consumption. The larger species were taken to market slung on rings or twine; the smaller were packed in baskets.

5.   BOATS AND SHIPS

Josephus states that there were over 4,000 boats, skiffs, barges, and other craft on the Lake in his time.[3] Besides the fishing vessels, there were ferry-boats for passengers and goods. The Roman garrison at Tiberias had a fleet of small war-ships. We have no definite knowledge of the type of fishing boats, but as the size and build of fishing vessels is mainly dependent on the gear used, the species caught, and the particular locality, it may be presumed that the Galilean fishing craft two thousand years ago were about the same size as those found to-day. For the seine and cast-nets are still the normal means of capture. Boats built

---

[1] *Op. cit.*, p. 292.
[2] Cf. F. Delitzch, *Jewish Artisan Life*, p. 33.
[3] *Life*, 32, 33; *Wars*, II, 21, 8–10. A sea fight on the Lake is described in *Wars*, III, 10, 1, 5, 6, 9.

for these methods of fishing must not have too much draught as they have to be run in on to the beach. Again, they must not be too heavy, for if there is no wind, oars have to be used. Sometimes artists depict Galilean fishing boats in the time of Christ almost as large as Roman merchantmen of that date; this is incorrect. We may be certain that there was a single mast with a square sail. The lateen sail, now so common all round the Mediterranean, and found on the Sea of Galilee, was not introduced until the Middle Ages.[1] The only detail of a boat mentioned in the Gospels is the cushion in the stern on which Jesus fell asleep.

The modern fishing boats are of two main types: ordinary dinghies, and older double-ended craft.[2] In the latter the stern post has only a slight rake. The stem is curved—rather like the stem in the now obsolete Scottish " Scaffie ", once common on the Moray Firth. In some of these boats the stem-post projects several inches above the gunwale. All have a shallow draught, and most are very beamy, with an average length of from 15 to 20 feet. Wooden thole-pins are used when rowing. The oars are square in the loom, and very heavy. It is a common sight to see the Arab fishermen standing to their oars when rowing. The mast is fixed about two-thirds of the distance from stern to stem. Both fore and aft there is a small decked-in space; the latter being used

[1] The lateen took the place of the square sail wherever the Moslems gained control, whether on the Indian Ocean or on the Mediterranean. It spread from the Aegean to the Atlantic and is " evidence of the influence which Mohammedanism has exercised upon modern navigation in these waters " (H. Warrington Smyth, *Mast and Sail in Europe and Asia*, p. 285).
[2] Since World War II it seems that all Galilean fishing boats have had motors installed.

to stow the net when the crew are not fishing. As has been already stated, a lateen sail is used. A normal crew consists of four men.

Hand-nets are used all over the Lake. Seine or drag-nets are mainly confined to the northern end. The hand-nets are circular in shape, with a very fine mesh, weighted by a dozen or so small lumps of lead.[1]

In the late spring of 1929, I spent a week by the Sea of Galilee, and was able to visualize almost every incident connected with fishing and fishermen recorded in the Gospels. I watched them returning to land in the early morning, bringing their catch ashore, sorting it, and putting it up for sale. I stood over the fishermen while they were cleaning and washing their nets. At nightfall I would see them putting out to sea. At Tiberias, where I enjoyed the hospitality of the Franciscans, is the old church dedicated to St. Peter the Fisherman. The rough exterior resembles the stern of an upturned boat. From the windows of my room, or from the roof of the Pilgrims' Hospice, I could gaze over the waters of the Lake.

Day after day the sun poured down. The sky was an unclouded blue, the surface of the Lake motionless, except for an occasional dark patch when a puff of wind rippled the waters. The heavy, sultry heat, not to mention the smells, was an ever present reminder of the atmosphere to which Christ and his disciples must have been so accustomed that they hardly noticed it. But in their time there would have been the even more penetrating odours of fish curing. These would have been a mixture of that sickly smell of the sardine ports of Brittany or Portugal, where the

[1] For details of seine-nets, see pp. 53, 54.

air is filled with the fumes of boiling oil; and the
briny smell common to ports on the east coast of
Britain where herring is gutted and packed in salt;
or the acrid fumes of kippering as the same fish is
smoked over wood-shavings.

Then, quite suddenly, on my last morning, there
came a storm of wind, and the waves began to break
against the wooden jetty of Tiberias. Practically all
the fishermen were at home, for they had been out the
previous night. In a few minutes, after the first gust
of wind, they were dashing along the streets towards
the pier. By this time the surface of the Lake was
covered with white-crested waves. The wind had
risen to almost the force of a gale. The sky had
turned from pale blue to dark grey.

The fishermen flung off their clothes, except for
their shirts, and dived off the jetty. They swam out
to their boats, clambered aboard, unloosed the mooring
ropes or hauled up the anchors, and next I saw them
standing to their oars, rowing hard, with the spray
blowing against their faces. They were making for
the small harbour which lies about a quarter of a
mile north of Tiberias.

It was exciting to watch them. Seldom had I ever
seen men handling boats with such skill. For the
moment I forgot that they were rowing on an inland
lake, for the grey-green water and the angry little
waves might have been the open sea off a low sandy
shore. By the time the last of the boats had made
the harbour, the wind dropped, and in less than half
an hour the storm had spent itself. Such an incident
as this must have been a common event in the lives
of Peter, Andrew, James and John.[1]

[1]Cf. P. F. Anson, *Fishermen and Fishing Ways,* pp. 20–28.

6. THE SEA OF GALILEE AND ITS ASSOCIATIONS
WITH JESUS

It is a curious fact that none of the places around the Sea of Galilee with which our Lord was associated so intimately during the three years of his active ministry has been regarded as worthy of preservation. There is not even a memorial or tradition of most of them. " The Christian Church seems hardly to have made an effort to seek or to recover what ought to have been its historical sanctuaries on these wonderful shores."[1] This neglect was partly due to the attention fixed on the Nativity and Death rather than on the Life and Works of Christ.

" Jesus used to go and come from one side to another, together with His disciples, to spread the knowledge of His teaching and miracles along its shores. There the barque of Peter, assailed one day by a violent gale, seemed on the point of sinking, when at the command of Jesus the wind suddenly dropped and the sea became calm. The boat of Peter, which in the end happily made port, has become the figure of the Church (see Matthew 8.23–27; Luke 8.23–25).

" On its waves Jesus walked towards His disciples, as if He were on solid and firm ground. Peter, full of confidence in the all-powerfulness of his Master, asked to be allowed to do the same (see Matthew 14.22–32).

" It was also from a barque that the Divine Master spoke to the crowd assembled on the shore, and explained to them the parables of the kingdom of heaven (see Luke 5.1–9).

" Its waters also witnessed many miraculous draughts of fishes. The first was followed by the call of the

[1] Stanley, *Sinai and Palestine*, p. 385.

Apostles (Matthew 4.18–22, and John 1.35, 44). The second was used for the payment of the tax for the Master and for the Prince of the Apostles (see Matthew 17.23–26). On the occasion of the third, which took place after the resurrection of Our Saviour, Peter was instituted Vicar of Jesus Christ upon earth.

" As one advances along its shores the holy lake ever evokes new memories, which in a striking manner recall the familiar figure of Christ upon its waters."[1]

7.   TOWNS AND VILLAGES

Somewhere on the west side of the Lake, four miles either to the north or south of Tiberias, lay the prosperous town of Tericheae, which is not mentioned in the Gospels. It was the chief fish-curing centre—the name means " pickling places "—and ship-building was another important industry. The harbour was a safe refuge for vessels.

Tiberias, founded in A.D. 21 by Herod Antipas, Tetrarch of Galilee, was mainly a Roman garrison town, a pagan centre and as such avoided by the Jews. It was famous for its hot springs and bathing establishments. The modern town was built by the Crusaders. The ancient city, the walls of which were at least three miles in circumference, extended northwards. Violent earthquakes in the past have destroyed even the ruins.

Magdala was situated about four miles north of Tiberias. It was a centre for dyers and weavers, but also had a fisher quarter. The people were regarded as very corrupt.

Capharnaum has also vanished completely, and archaeologists are still undecided where it lay. Some are of opinion that this great town was situated at

[1] Meistermann, *New Guide to the Holy Land*, pp. 535, 536.

the north end of the Plain of Genesareth, where the highway from Damascus to the Mediterranean reached the shores of the Lake; others argue that Capharnaum occupied the site of Tell Houm, about three miles farther east, where the ruins of an ancient synagogue have been discovered. They maintain that this was the identical synagogue built by the Roman centurion mentioned in the Gospels, and in which our Lord preached.

Perhaps it will never be decided where Capharnaum was situated; anyhow, somewhere along this shore was the second home of Jesus.

In the end, Jesus would pronounce a curse on this town, as on other places beside the Lake: " And I say this, that it shall go less hard with the country of Sodom at the day of judgment than with thee."[1]

Bethsaida, which means " House of the Fishers " or " Fisher Town ", has also disappeared from the face of the earth. All we know for certain is that it was situated in the country of Genesareth.[2] " The House of the Fishers " was the native place of Andrew, Peter and Philip.[3]

The site of Bethsaida is a vexed question.[4] It is possible that there were two places of the same name, each situated at the head of the Sea of Galilee, and deriving their name from the shoals of fish drawn to both spots by the hot springs flowing into the Lake:

1.   *Ain Tabigah*—about two miles east of the Plain of Genesareth, a rocky cove, which may well have been a fishing village and the home of Andrew, Peter, James and John, also the scene of the miraculous

---

[1] Matthew 11.23–24.
[2] Mark 6.45, 53.
[3] John 1.44.
[4] See note, p. 29.

draughts of fishes. For nearly sixteen hundred years this stretch of the shore was always pointed out to pilgrims as the site of Bethsaida.

2. *Et-Tell*—on the east of the Jordan. Josephus mentions this Bethsaida. The original village was rebuilt by Philip the Tetrarch, and the city renamed Julias in honour of the daughter of the Emperor Augustus. According to some authorities, it was somewhere to the south of Julias that Christ fed the five thousand. However, it was not until early in the seventeenth century that this opinion was brought forward.

It is more probable that the miracle of the feeding of the five thousand took place in a desert place among the hills behind the first-named Bethsaida. The controversy mainly rests on the precise meaning of the words "*trans fretum*"—beyond, to the other side. This need not necessarily mean crossing from one side of the lake to the other, but from one promontory or point to the next, since the shore consists of a series of small bays. Anyhow, what we have said about the site of Bethsaida merely proves how little effort was made by the early Christians to preserve even the memory of the sacred spots on the Sea of Galilee.

8. THE SEA OF GALILEE IN THE TIME OF CHRIST

It is hard to form a mental picture of what the Sea of Galilee must have been like two thousand years ago, for the conditions were so utterly different from what they are to-day. Along its northern shores was the great thoroughfare leading from Babylon and Damascus to the Mediterranean. The Roman villas, set in their rich gardens, " must have given to the lake a beauty which we are accustomed to consider as peculiar to the shores of Como or Lugano ".[1] There were many prosperous towns and villages which " sent forth their fishermen by hundreds over the lake; and when we add the crowds of ship-builders, the many boats of traffic, pleasure and passage, we see the whole basin must have been a focus of life and energy; the surface of the lake constantly dotted with the white sails of vessels, flying before the mountain gusts as the beach sparkled with the houses and palaces, the synagogues, and the temples of the Jewish or Roman inhabitants ".[2]

There were the docks and harbour at Tericheae, as H. V. Morton reminds us, with their " long rows of sheds, the sound of hammers as coopers barrelled fish, the noise of ship-building ".[3] Greek and Latin were spoken in the towns as well as Aramaic. The Jews mixed with the Gentile races. It was a world of ceaseless toil by land and on the waters.

" The heathen or half-heathen ' publicans ' or tax-gatherers would be there, sitting by the lakeside ' at the receipt of custom '. The ' women who were sinners ' would have come there, either from the neighbouring Gentile cities, or corrupted by the licence of Gentile manners. The Roman soldiers would there be found quartered with their slaves, to be near the palaces of the Herodian princes, or to repress the turbulence of the Galilean peasantry. And the hardy boatmen, filled with the faith and grateful spirit by which that peasantry was always distinguished, would supply the energy and docility which were needed for His followers. The copious fisheries of the lake

---

[1] Stanley, *Sinai and Palestine*, p. 375.
[2] *Ibid.*, p. 376.
[3] *Op. cit.*, p. 220.

now assumed a new interest. The two boats by the beach; Simon and Andrew casting their nets into the water; James and John on the shore washing and mending their nets; the ' toiling all the night and catching nothing '; ' the great multitude of fishes so that the net brake '; Philip, Andrew, and Simon from ' Bethsaida ', the ' House of the Fisheries '; the ' casting a hook for the first fish that cometh up '; the ' net cast into the sea, and gathering of every kind '—all these things could occur nowhere else in Palestine but on this one spot, and which from that one spot have now passed into the religious language of the civilised world, and in their remotest applications, or even misapplications, have converted the nations and shaken the thrones of Europe."[1]

Passing to and fro amid the cosmopolitan crowds of the towns and villages around the Sea of Galilee—a world in some ways not unlike that which still exists on the French and Italian Rivieras—Jesus became a familiar figure for the greater part of three years. We can visualize him standing on the shore, gazing over the waters of the Lake; boarding a boat, moored by the rocks, and bidding Peter launch out into deeper water. Crowds never ceased to follow this famous preacher; so great were they that he had to escape from them on the water, not once but again and again. Those three years of the active ministry of Christ were bound up with fishermen, fishing and fishing boats. It must be made clear that it was no quiet and peaceful mountain lake where nature is undisturbed by the presence of man, but a busy coast-line, where the commercial and maritime activity was almost unique in the world of that date. Sailors, soldiers, merchants,

[1] Stanley, *op. cit.*, pp. 377–78.

travellers, messengers, officers, princes, men of many classes and from many parts of the world, passed through these ports on business or on pleasure.

Jesus chose to make his home there for those three years on the road to the sea that led from Syria to the Mediterranean, one of the main highways of the Roman Empire. Among the fishermen of the towns he found the type of men he most needed for his inner circle of disciples. " Christ went to a trade which had no private wrongs, and called men, not from their dreams, but from work they were contented to do from day to day until something higher should touch them. And so it came to pass that not the jargon of the fanatics and brigands in the Highlands of Galilee, but the speech of the fishermen of her lake, and the instruments of their simple craft, have become the language and symbolism of the world's religion."[1]

It was in the midst of this world of fishermen and fish workers, and all the many subsidiary industries connected with the catching, selling, curing and export of fish, that Christianity arose, and Christ himself carried on most of his apostolate. For this reason it is important that we should try to visualize and understand it. The same world exists, as it has done in all ages, in every part of the maritime world. For a particular kind of work forms a particular type of people, no matter to what race they belong. They think about, and talk about, the same matters connected with their job. Nor can their home-life have been very different from that which we find in any typical fisher community, granting different climates and local customs and traditions. Just as the majority

[1] G. A. Smith, *op. cit.*, p. 463.

of French, Italian, Spanish and Portuguese fishermen are still devout, practising Catholics, regular in their attendance at Sunday Mass, whenever they happen to be ashore; or the Scottish fishermen, for the greater part, equally loyal in their attendance at the kirk, or the meetings of one or other of the innumerable Protestant sects which abound in their ports, so too were the Galilean fishermen, orthodox Jews, who attended the services at their local synagogues on the Sabbath, and who, just like so many of our own fisher folk, were eager to listen to any wandering evangelist who would expound the Word of God to them. So it is not really surprising that the four most intimate disciples of our Lord should have been fishermen. To anybody who has lived among fishermen and been accepted by them, it would be almost surprising if he had chosen his inner circle of followers from any other class of men.

NOTE

There has been much controversy in recent years over the site of Bethsaida. George Adam Smith (*The Historical Geography of the Holy Land*, p. 457) is convinced that there was a Bethsaida (" Fisher-Home ") on the east bank of the Jordan, near the mouth of the river. It was near here that the miracle of the feeding of the five thousand took place. He doubts if there was another Bethsaida. Edersheim (*The Life and Times of Jesus the Messiah*, Vol. II, p. 3) thinks it much more likely that there were at least two towns or villages of this same name. " Remembering how common the corresponding name—' Fisherton '—is in our own country, and that fishing was the main industry of the Lake, we need not wonder at the existence of more than one Bethsaida, or ' Fisherton '. Nor yet does it seem strange, that the site should have been lost of what, probably, except for the fishing, was quite an unimportant place. By the testimony both of Josephus and the Rabbis, the shores of Genesareth were thickly studded with little towns, villages and hamlets, which have all perished without leaving a trace, while even the largest of the ruins are few and inconsiderable." Edersheim concludes that one of these Bethsaidas was merely the fishing quarter of Capharnaum: " even as we so often find in our own country a ' Fisherton ' adjacent to larger towns ".

CHAPTER III

CHRIST'S APOSTOLATE AMONG THE GALILEAN FISHERMEN

CHRIST'S APOSTOLATE AMONG THE GALILEAN FISHERMEN

So when they brought their boats to land, they left all and followed him—Luke 5.11.

He came and settled down in Capharnaum, which is by the sea shore—Matthew 4.13.

Peter answered him: " Lord, if it is thyself, bid me come to thee over the water "—Matthew 14.28.

JONA, a fisherman of Bethsaida, had two sons whose names were Simon and Andrew. The name of their native village means " The Fisherman's Home " or " Fishertown ". Jona seems to have been fairly prosperous, for he owned at least one boat. As has been pointed out already, there is such a startling similarity in the background of fisher-life in almost every country, that it is not very difficult to form a mental picture of the childhood and youth of these two sons of Jona of Bethsaida. As soon as they could walk, they would have been playing about on the beach or wanting to be taken down to the place where their father's boat was moored. As they grew older they would have amused themselves catching fish from the rocks with improvised rods and lines. Doubtless they made model boats, and sailed them on the lake. They wore very few clothes in that hot climate, and spent long hours paddling or bathing. Then they went to school. Here they would have been taught Hebrew, to enable them to take their part in the worship of the synagogue. In their home, Aramaic

33

was the language spoken. It is more than likely that they soon picked up a smattering of Greek, for the merchants and fish-buyers were mainly Gentiles from distant islands and far-off countries. Soldiers, especially if they are on foreign service and cut off from a family life of their own, tend to fraternize with boys, and what boys would be able to resist the glamour of those Roman uniforms worn by the garrison which kept guard over the turbulent Galileans? Perhaps Simon played with a sword many years before he cut off the ear of Malchus, the servant of the High Priest. Very likely he and his younger brother, Andrew, listened to the soldiers talking Latin and could understand bits of their conversation. But Greek was the *lingua franca* of the Roman Empire by this date, and Galilee was part of that Empire.

To judge by what we know of Simon's character in after years, he must have been a wild, high-spirited, outspoken lad; eager for any adventure, boastful and conceited, yet at the same time generous to anybody who won his affection. It is obvious that he was the leader of a gang of fisher lads, who carried on in much the same way as fisher lads do in any part of the world. Had those Aramaic oaths and blasphemies which sprung to his lips when he lost his head and swore that he had never heard of Jesus, merely been buried in his subconsciousness from the days of his youth, when, like any normal lad, he was eager to prove that he was a man, and able to swear as well as any adult fisherman?

Having left school, Simon and Andrew would have started to earn their living in one or other of their father's boats. From childhood they had been familiar with everything to do with fishing. They could handle an oar, manage a boat under sail, knew how to watch for those dark patches on the lake which indicated a squall of wind, and how to mend nets. They could knot and splice ropes. Every species of fish caught on the lake would be known to them, and not only the fish, but the prices at which they were sold. The fishermen had told them where the shoals were most often located, and what were the landmarks for picking up these grounds. All their interests centred around the lake and its fishing industry: it was their life.

We know that Simon was married, and considering his character it is more than probable that it was not long before he was betrothed to a young girl from the same district, and probably of the same fisher class, for nowhere is it usual for a fisherman to take a wife from the country. The betrothal ceremony among the Galileans was a more simple affair than in other parts of Judaea. The legal details of dowries of the future husband and wife had to be settled, and other mutual obligations. A year or longer may have elapsed before Simon was married. The night before the marriage ceremony, his bride was led along the streets of Bethsaida from her own home to that of her husband. Other fishermen, dressed in their best clothes, were among the crowd who carried torches or lamps on poles. After the rite had been performed, and Simon and his wife crowned with garlands of flowers, he signed a document undertaking to support, honour, keep and care for her. Then began the marriage feast, prolonged until late that night, or until the small hours of the following morning. The Evangelists do not state whether Simon had any children, neither do they mention his wife, only his

mother-in-law.   St. Clement of Alexandria, who lived
in the second century after Christ, records a tradition
that St. Peter had children, and that his wife suffered
martyrdom.

Both Simon and Andrew must have been devout
young men, otherwise they would not have felt it
worth while to give up fishing to journey from the
Sea of Galilee to the banks of the Jordan to listen to
the preaching of John the Baptist, no matter how
great was the notoriety of this prophet.   This proves
that both of them took an interest in religion as well
as in their profession.

James and John, the two other fishermen who
became the disciples of Jesus, were the sons of Zebedee
and Salome.   Like Jona, the father of Simon and
Andrew, Zebedee was a well-to-do fisherman and
boat-owner on the Sea of Galilee.   He probably lived
at Bethsaida or Capharnaum.   Salome, in later years,
was one of the devout women who followed Christ
and " ministered unto him of their substance ".[1]   We
know nothing of the early years of James or John.
Their boyhood and youth were doubtless passed in
much the same way as that of Simon and Andrew.
It is possible that Salome was a sister of Mary, the
Mother of Jesus; if so, then this would make James
and John first cousins of our Lord, but the relationship
is doubtful.

Both brothers must have been hot-tempered, otherwise our Lord would not have given them the
nickname of " Sons of Thunder ".   This vehemence
of character was common among Galileans of all
classes.   Taken as a whole, they were brave, in-
dustrious, religious, and strongly nationalist in their

[1] Matthew 27.55; Mark 15.40; Luke 8.2.

outlook.   Zebedee's two sons worked in partnership with Simon and Andrew.   All four fished with Zebedee and his hired men.   John may have been a "son of thunder", but a study of the Gospel he wrote in after years is enough to prove that he was of a deeply spiritual mentality, a far stronger character than Simon.   It was he who would bring his brother James to the Messias, after Andrew had taken the lead and become the first disciple.   Very likely these four fishermen made the journey together from Galilee to the Jordan to hear John the Baptist.

I.   THE FIRST CALL OF THE FISHERMEN-APOSTLES

John 1.35–42:

The next day after this, John was standing there again, with two of his disciples; and, watching Jesus as he walked by, he said, " Look, this is the Lamb of God ".   The two disciples heard him say it, and they followed Jesus.   Turning, and seeing them follow him, Jesus asked, " What would you have of me? "   " Rabbi," they said (a word which means Master), " where dost thou live? "   He said to them, " Come and see "; so they went and saw where he lived, and they stayed with him all the rest of the day, from about the tenth hour onwards.   One of the two who had heard what John said, and followed him, was Andrew, the brother of Simon Peter.   He, first of all, found his own brother, Simon, and told him, " We have discovered the Messias! " (which means the Christ), and brought him to Jesus.   Jesus looked at him closely, and said, " Thou art Simon the son of Jona; thou shalt be called Cephas " (which means the same as Peter).

Two young fishermen, Andrew and John, having heard of a new religious teacher, whom men called

John the Baptist, undertook the long journey from the Sea of Galilee to the valley of the Jordan. It seems that they were converted by his sermons, and were probably baptized. They stayed on for a while forming part of a group of disciples.

One day while the Baptist was speaking to the crowd, he noticed a man standing some distance away. Some of those present may have recognized this figure as the same individual at whose baptism, some time before, the heavens had opened, and a voice was heard, saying: "This is my Beloved Son, in whom I am well pleased."

The Precursor looked at him, and turning to the crowd, said, "Behold the Lamb of God!" The two fishermen realized that this stranger could be no other than the long-expected Messias. Maybe they had already heard that he had been preaching through Galilee and Judaea. Anyhow, they left John the Baptist and made their way to where Jesus was standing. No doubt they were shy, and did not quite know how to begin a conversation. So they asked the obvious question, just what any young man might put to a stranger: "Master, where do you live?"

The three walked off together. Jesus took them to where he was lodging. It would have been difficult to find quiet and peace among the crowds. They spent several hours with their new friend, engaged in earnest conversation. There was something different about this new Master from John the Baptist: a sympathy, an affectionateness, perhaps? Whatever it was, the two Galilean fishermen were conquered.

Fired with enthusiasm and eager to make another convert, Andrew rushed off to find his brother, Simon.

Having done so, he brought him to Jesus, telling him that he and John had discovered the Messias. Jesus looked at this third fisherman closely: he was unlike the others. Then he said: " Simon, son of Jona; I am going to give you a nickname, and call you Cephas, which means a rock! " This remark, which must have struck Peter as a joke, if he had any self-knowledge and realized his natural instability, had the result of making him throw in his lot with the Messias.

The following day Jesus left the valley of the Jordan and set out for Galilee. No doubt he was accompanied by his three fishermen converts, who felt they must be getting back to their jobs. When they got home he met another native of the port of Bethsaida, by name Philip. Like Andrew, John and Simon he decided to become one of the disciples of Jesus.

What strikes one most on reading this story, is that it might have happened in our own times instead of nearly two thousand years ago. Andrew and John have so much in common with many a young seafarer or fisherman; you find their type in almost every maritime community in almost any country . . . young men of the middle-class, well brought up, who find an outlet in religion, instead of in sport. None of those Galilean fishermen converts was poor. Their families were comfortably off, proud of their profession, and devout observers of religious duties. You can discover Andrew, John and Simon among twentieth-century fisher families. They exist among the " *militants* " of the Young Christian Seafarers in France; they are just as common among the non-Catholic fisher folk of many Protestant denominations on the North and East coasts of Scotland; they will be found in many a Seamen's Club in almost any part of the world. The type persists among those who follow the sea.[1]

2.   JESUS MAKES HIS SECOND HOME AMONG A FISHER COMMUNITY

Matthew 4.13–17:

And now, forsaking the city of Nazareth, he came and settled down in Capharnaum, which is by the sea shore, in the country of Zabulon and Nephthalim, in fulfilment of what was said by the prophet Isaias: The land of Zabulon and Nephthalim on the sea road, beyond Jordan, the Galilee of the Gentiles! The people that abode in darkness has seen a great light; for men abiding in a land where death over-shadowed them, light has dawned. From that time onwards, Jesus began to preach: " Repent," he said, " the kingdom of heaven is at hand."

Luke 4.29–31:

They rose and thrust him out of the city . . . but he passed through the midst of them, and so went on his way. Then he went down to Capharnaum, which is a city in Galilee, and began teaching them there on the sabbath; and they were

[1] According to certain philologists the word apostle has a remote connection with the sea. They are of the opinion that more than two thousand years ago Greek sailors began to use the word *apostólos* as an adjective qualifying *ploion*, when they wanted to refer to a cargo ship. As time went on " sea slang " dropped the noun and retained the original adjective, when mentioning the equivalent of a modern tramp steamer. One may presume that the crews of the Greek warships, commanded by Themistocles, who defeated the Persian squadron in the Battle of Salamis (480 B.C.), spoke of a certain type of vessel as *apostólos*. By degrees the word began to imply a fleet of ships, and then was restricted to the leader of a fleet, i.e., an admiral or captain. It was the sending out that mattered, not the nature of the commission. In Greek the verb *apostéllein* was often used to denote the sending out of a fleet. So when we use the word apostle to-day, we refer to what once meant a cargo ship! (Cf. K. H. Rengstorf, *Apostleship*, Bible Key Words from Gerhard Kittel's *Theologisches Wörterbuch zum Neun Testament* (1952), pp. 1–3.)

*amazed at his teaching, such was the authority with which
he spoke.*

John 2.12:

*After that he went down to Capharnaum with his mother,
his brethren, and his disciples, not staying there many days.*

It is significant that Jesus not only chose fishermen
as his first Apostles, but when he was driven out of
Nazareth, he made his new home in the chief centre of
the fishing industry in Palestine.   More than this, he
lodged with a fisher family.   The carpenter from a hill-
town, regarded suspiciously at first as an " incomer ",
might have been absorbed into the life of the seafaring
community without much attention, had he not immediately obtained notoriety as an itinerant evangelist.
But he gathered crowds around him on the shore and
in the streets, while he talked to them about the need
for repentance and the imminence of the kingdom of
heaven.   On the sabbath he preached in the synagogues, where the congregations were amazed at his
knowledge of the Scriptures and the authority with
which he spoke.   Moreover, it would appear that, after
Jesus had been expelled from his native town, his
Mother and some of her relatives followed him to
Capharnaum and settled in this busy city, which lay
on the high-road from Damascus to the Mediterranean.
Nazareth was a peaceful backwater; Capharnaum
was the hub of the universe in comparison.

Nowhere else did our Lord pronounce so many
discourses or perform so many miracles.   From its
Customs House, hard by the quays, he called Matthew
as his sixth Apostle.   Here he bade Peter cast a hook
into the Lake to catch a fish in whose mouth he would
find a silver coin to pay the tax for the Temple at

Jerusalem. In a house in this city he raised to life the daughter of Jairus, the head of the synagogue. A pagan centurion gave an example of rare humility to the onlookers, somewhere within sound of the lapping of the waves on the shore. It was on the flat roof of one of the houses in the fisher quarter that the paralytic man was let down in his bed. One sabbath morning, when, no doubt, many fishermen were gathered in the synagogue, our Lord cured another man, in this instance one possessed by an unclean spirit. As he walked along the crowded streets a woman suffering from an issue of blood was cured by touching the hem of his garment. In the house of Peter, Jesus cured the fisherman's mother-in-law of a violent fever. One evening, after sunset, crowds gathered before this house, bringing to Jesus persons who were sick in body or in mind. The boats put out to sea as it grew dark, and the lights began to twinkle over the Lake, but the Healer continued his work of mercy, even casting out many devils. Then, worn out by this terrific strain, he slipped away to a lonely place in the adjacent hills. In the grey dawn he would have made out the boats hauling in their nets before they returned to port. These and other incidents took place during the three years of our Lord's active ministry, when his home was among the fisher folk of Capharnaum. He was not resident there for long at a time: he came and went, just as the boats did. Capharnaum was his " home port ". Just as the sun rose over the mountain ranges on the far side of the Lake, so the people of Capharnaum " that abode in darkness had seen a great light ". For these men and women were abiding with the threat of spiritual death overshadowing them. The light dawning in their midst found none so quick as the fisher folk to take to heart the message of repentance and believe that the kingdom of heaven was actually at hand.

The first Christian community seems to have been established at Capharnaum about the middle of the fourth century. The Emperor Constantine built a church in what pilgrims of that date supposed were the ruins of a church erected by St. Peter. These ruins are now recognized to be those of a synagogue, probably erected by a Roman centurion before the destruction of Jerusalem in A.D. 70. There is little doubt that it was in this synagogue on the shore of the lake that Jesus and his Apostles worshipped, and where he often preached.

3. THE FOUR FISHERMEN LEAVE THEIR CAST-NETS TO FOLLOW JESUS

Matthew 4.18-22:

As he walked by the sea of Galilee, Jesus saw two brethren, Simon, who is called Peter, and his brother Andrew, casting a net into the sea (for they were fishermen). He said to them: " Come and follow me; I will make you into fishers of men."

They dropped their nets immediately, and followed him.

Then he went further on, and saw two others that were brethren, James the son of Zebedee and his brother John. They were in the boat with their father, Zebedee, repairing their nets, and he called them to him. Whereupon they dropped their nets and left their father immediately, and followed him.

Mark 1.16-20:

As he passed along the sea of Galilee, he saw Simon and Simon's brother Andrew casting a net into the sea (for they were fishermen). Jesus said to them: " Come and follow me; I will make you fishers of men." They dropped their nets immediately and followed him.

Then he went a little further, and saw James, the son of Zebedee, and his brother John; these two were in their boat, repairing their nets. All at once he called them, and they, leaving their father Zebedee in the boat with the hired men, turned aside after him.

Most commentators are of the opinion that St. Luke's description of the final calling of the fishermen-Apostles is merely a more detailed version of that given in Matthew 4 and Mark 1. A fisherman comparing these three stories would probably notice that both Matthew and Mark seem to refer to a cast-net being used from the shore, whereas there is no doubt that Luke describes a seine or drag-net, shot from a boat, at some distance from the land. There is also the reference to " toiling all night ". Cast-nets are mainly used in daylight. So a fisherman who studies the differences in the gear used in these three narratives would prefer to think that our Lord may have told Simon and Andrew that they would be " fishers of men " on more than one occasion. So we will not attempt to combine the incident related with such graphic detail by St. Luke with the much briefer story narrated by St. Matthew and St. Mark, the details of which are practically identical.

They give us a picture of Jesus walking along the beach, with no indication of the time of day, and coming to a spot where Simon and Andrew were casting a net into the sea. H. V. Morton thus describes the method of using a cast-net:[1]

[1] *In the Steps of the Master*, p. 198.

" We beached the boat in a desolate little bay. One of the fishermen girded his garments to the waist and waded into the lake with his nets draped over his left arm. He stood waiting, as if watching for a movement in the water. Then, with a swift over-arm motion, he cast the hand-net. It shot through the air and descended on the water like a ballet dancer's skirt when she sinks to the ground. The dozens of little lead weights carried the bell-shaped net through the water, imprisoning any fish within its area.

" But time after time the net came up empty. It was a beautiful sight to see him casting. Each time the neatly folded net belled out in the air and fell so precisely on the water that the small lead weights hit the lake at the same moment, making a thin circular splash."

It may be a long time before the fisherman strikes a shoal of fish. Very often another man—no doubt Andrew in the Gospel story—remains on the shore and notices the fish in the water before they are visible to his partner. Then he will shout to the other and tell him where to cast the net.

Taking the two narratives as they stand, the story is quite simple. Simon and Andrew are casting their nets; the former standing in the water, the latter watching from the shore. Jesus passes by and tells them to follow him. They drop their nets at once and leave them on the beach. We are not informed whether they had caught any fish; all that is stated is that Jesus told the two brothers that he would make them " fishers of men ", and that they followed him as he continued his walk along the shore.

Then comes the second incident: within a few minutes Jesus sees a boat, moored in a rocky cove, or

in the shallow water of one of those sandy beaches
which alternate on the coast near the traditional site
of Bethsaida. In this boat are fishermen mending
their nets. (Both the seine and cast-nets used on the
Sea of Galilee easily get torn, for the mesh is very fine.)
Jesus calls two of the men by name: James and John.
They drop their wooden needles, the balls of twine,
the nets they are repairing, and without a moment's
hesitation, leave their father, Zebedee, with the hired
men who formed the rest of the crew. Either wading
through the water or clambering over the rocks, they
hasten to where Jesus is standing with Simon and
Andrew. Then the four fishermen walk away along
the shore, most likely towards Capharnaum, where
Jesus has now made his home since he was driven out
of Nazareth. Zebedee and his crew watch them as
they pass out of sight, while they stay and finish off
the mending of the nets. What did they have to say
about this strange behaviour of the four young fishermen? If you think of it from the point of view of
the ordinary fisherman, it was hardly the thing to
abandon a good job without giving notice, merely
because an itinerant preacher had given them a call.
Simon and Andrew left their nets; James and John
left their father's boat. He would have to find two
other men to take to fill their berths, and pay them
wages. Did anybody pick up those nets that Simon
and his brother dropped on the beach in such a hurry?
Nets cost money, and it merely shows how impetuous
was Simon, that he should not have thought of taking
the nets with him when he followed his new Master.
Even if he did not intend to use them any more, the
nets could have been sold. James and John, " the
Sons of Thunder ", do not seem to have thought of

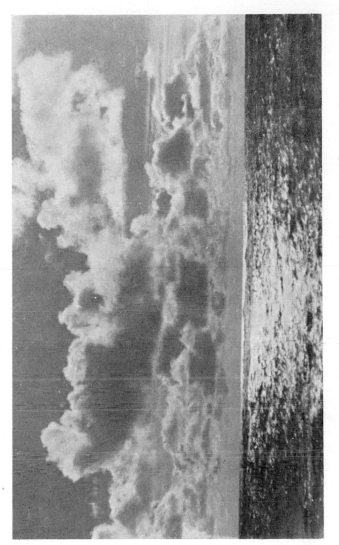

" And the spirit of God moved over the waters " [*Genesis 1.2*]

" Thy way is in the sea, and thy paths in many waters " [*Psalm 76.20*]

the inconvenience they were giving to their father by walking out on him.

4.   THE LAST CALL OF THE FISHERMEN-APOSTLES,
        AND THE MIRACLE OF THE SEINE-NET

Luke 5.1–11 :

It happened that Jesus was standing by the lake of Genesareth, at a time when the multitude was pressing close about him to hear the word of God.   He saw two boats moored at the edge of the lake; the fishermen had gone ashore, and were washing their nets.

He went on board one of the boats, which belonged to Simon, and asked him to stand off a little from the land; and so, sitting down, he began to teach the multitudes from the boat.

When he had finished speaking, he said to Simon, " Stand out into the deep water, and let down your nets for a catch." Simon answered him, " Master, we have toiled all the night, and caught nothing; but at thy word I will let down the net."

When they had done this, they took a great quantity of fish, so that the net was near breaking, and they must needs beckon to their partners who were in the other boat to come and help them.   When these came, they filled both boats, so that they were ready to sink.

At seeing this, Simon Peter fell down and caught Jesus by the knees.   " Leave me to myself, Lord," he said: " I am a sinner."

Such amazement had overcome both him and all his crew, at the catch of fish they had made; so it was too, with James and John, the sons of Zebedee, who were Simon's partners. But Jesus said to Simon, " Do not be afraid, henceforth thou shalt be a fisher of men."

So, when they had brought their boats to land, they left all and followed him.

E

Crowds have assembled on the sea shore, hoping that Jesus will preach to them, although it is still very early in the morning. The people are forcing their way up to him, trying to attract his attention, wanting either help and advice, or to be healed of their diseases.

It has been a stormy night. Two boats are drawn up on the sandy beach between Bethsaida and Capharnaum. No fish has been caught. The nets have got torn and clogged with sand. The crews are washing them. The fishermen have gone ashore and are standing at the edge of the water. In order to escape from the crowds, Jesus goes aboard one of these boats which was owned by Simon. The men must have been weary after their night's fishing. They had no fish to sell that morning. No doubt they wanted to get home for a sleep. They may have been so intent on washing their nets that they did not notice Jesus among the crowds until he climbed into the boat.

Now he is well above the heads of the multitude. Peter's boat serves as an open-air pulpit, once its skipper has rowed out a few yards from the shore. Sitting down, Jesus begins to preach, and to teach the people by parables. The fishermen take up their nets, and sit around him in the boat, listening intently to his words.

When the discourse is ended, the sun is higher in the sky, and the morning well advanced. Jesus then turns to Simon, and bids him stand out into deeper water and let down his nets. This command must have surprised the crew, for fish are not usually caught in deep water after the sun has risen. Peter reminds Jesus that they have laboured all night and had no luck, but he has such confidence in his Master that he is ready to obey his orders. As to the rest of the crew, no doubt, subconsciously, they wonder what the " son of a carpenter " from a town among the hill-country could know about fishing, even if he was a remarkable preacher with an unusual knowledge of the Scriptures. They had doubtless seen him heal the sick of their diseases and perform other miracles, but this was a different matter. Even the crowds waiting on the shore may have wondered what was happening, for many of them would have known that it was far too late in the day to catch fish with drag-nets. Their attitude to the whole affair must have been not unlike that of twentieth-century Scottish herring fishermen if they saw a drifter shoot her fleet of nets in the forenoon. It is doubtful if any drifter skipper would have the faith of Peter, and say to a priest, parson, or preacher who had come aboard his vessel in the harbour: " Master, we have toiled all the night, and caught nothing, but at thy word I will let down the net." Onlookers would think that the skipper was just " daft " if he put to sea about eleven o'clock in the morning in the expectancy of finding a shoal of herring at a short distance from the land.

Anyhow, even if it was a mad thing to do, the men took to their oars and rowed out further into the Lake. The nets were shot from the stern of the boat, in the usual manner; but here is an interesting detail: St. Luke, always so careful in his maritime descriptions, implies that the nets were hauled in from the boats, not on the shore as is the normal method when using seine or drag-nets on the Sea of Galilee.   He mentions that the " net was near breaking " with the " great quantity of fish ".   Peter and his crew shouted to " their partners who were in the other boat to come and help them ".   Zebedee told his sons, James and

John, and the rest of the crew to row up hard, and
when they came alongside Peter's boat they lent a
hand in hauling in the net. There was so much fish
that one boat could not hold the catch. Peter's boat
was filled almost to the gunwale, and then Zebedee's,
with the result that both " were ready to sink ".

Peter was terrified. A shoal of fish was not anything
abnormal in itself; but what he and the other men
must have realized was that it needed supernatural
powers for a man to see through the waters, and know
that fish could be caught in a particular spot at a time
of day when they would not normally be found.
Like all Jews, Peter would have believed that to see
God was to die. Only God could have performed
such a miracle. The fisherman fell down at the feet
of his Master, saying, " Leave me to myself, Lord.
I am a sinner." The same terror overcame the other
men. Nothing like this had ever happened to them
before. They may have realized that this Rabbi saw
into the secret lives of everybody; that he could cure
diseases, change water into wine, and perform other
strange mysteries. But here was a supernatural
occurrence which touched them as no others had
done, just because it was directly concerned with their
occupation. They knew well enough that it was
difficult, if not impossible, to catch fish in this way.
After such a manifestation of divine power over nature,
they were prepared to do anything asked of them.

It is possible that, granted the incidents recorded
by Matthew and Mark refer to an occasion other than
that narrated by Luke, Peter and Andrew had returned
to their fishing after they had left their cast-nets on
the shore and followed Jesus. If so, then this
miraculous draught of fish was their final call to a

permanent discipleship. Hitherto these fishermen had been merely among the more regular disciples of Jesus, drawn closer and closer to him as he lured them with his bait. It was regarded as a sacred duty for a Rabbi to gather round him an inner circle of his disciples, so the call which was to be given was nothing unusual. These fishermen had already accepted Jesus as the Messias; perhaps they were already awaiting a sign to invite them to a much closer relationship with the Master?

" Come, follow me. I will make you fishers of men! " None of the four fishermen seems to have hesitated about obeying the call this time. It was a " clear call that may not be denied ", but in the opposite sense to that John Masefield implies in his poem " Sea Fever ". For in answering this call, Peter, Andrew, James and John would turn their backs on the " windy day with the white clouds flying, and the flung spray and the blown spume, and the sea-gulls crying ". They would ever recall the " grey mist on the sea's face and a grey dawn breaking " over the Lake of Genesareth. No more would they hear the " wind's song " and feel the " white sail's shaking ". The cold winds from snow-capped Hermon would not cut their faces " like a whetted knife ". They would look back, may be with regret, to those nights in the taverns of Capharnaum, with the

" merry yarn from a laughing fellow rover,
And quiet sleep and a sweet dream when the long
    trick's over."

So they got up, took the oars and rowed back to the shore. They had no choice: it was now clear that henceforth they were to catch the souls of men on dry land, and fish no more on the waters. They landed and went off with Jesus. Zebedee and the hired men remained in the boats, wondering, perhaps, what madness had seized the four others. If they were like the average fisherman, the first thing which they would have asked themselves would be: Is there any money to be made out of fishing for men? How would Peter support his wife and family? Of course he may have had private means.

We are not told if the four men who had answered the call went home to their families. Luke merely says: " They left all and followed Jesus." Later on our Lord would remind these fishermen that " if any man comes to me, without hating his father and mother and wife and children and brethren and sisters, yes, and his own life too, he can be no disciple of mine . . . none of you can be my disciples if he does not take leave of all that he possesses." That morning by the Sea of Galilee the four young fishermen took these words in their most literal sense, hardly realizing at the moment just what would be involved.

5.　THE PARABLE OF THE SEINE-NET

Matthew 13.47–50:

Again, the kingdom of heaven is like a net that was cast into the sea, and enclosed fish of every kind at once. When it was full the fishermen drew it up, and sat on the beach, where they stored all that was worth keeping in their buckets, and threw the useless kind away. So it will be when the world is brought to an end; the angels will go out and separate the wicked from the just, and will cast them into the furnace of fire, where there will be weeping, and gnashing of teeth.

Since there were so many fishermen who listened to Jesus preaching, it was only natural that he should choose at least one parable which had reference to their job. The type of net they often used on the Sea of Galilee was an obvious comparison for him to employ when trying to make them understand how good and evil must always exist side by side in this world, and how one day Divine Justice will separate the wicked from the just. We can picture Jesus telling this story, seated in a boat moored close to the shore, while the crowd stood on the beach, hanging on his words.

In much the same way, so Jesus pointed out to his hearers, do good and bad fish swim together until they are caught in God's net. At the end of the world his angels, like the fishermen, will sort out the good and bad " fish ". The latter will be cast, not into the sea, but into a " furnace of fire, where there will be weeping, and gnashing of teeth ".

It is obvious that a seine-net is visualized in this parable, for this was, and still is, one of the usual methods of fishing on the Sea of Galilee. The seine consists of a plain wall of netting, with corked head-lines and weighted foot-ropes. In some nets the mesh decreases in size towards the centre or " bunt ". Others have a sort of bag or " cod-end " in the centre to catch eels and smaller species of fish. The length varies, but an average short seine-net is from 60 to 80 yards on the rope. An average depth is 60 to 80 meshes of netting.

Shore-seines are worked as follows. The net is stowed on a boat. One end is attached to a rope, either held by men on shore or made fast to a pole. The boat is rowed out from the shore roughly in a semi-circle until all the net has been paid out. The boat is brought back to the shore, within a few yards of where it started. The crew come ashore. They catch hold of the end of the net left in the boat and haul in both ends. Thus all the fish are trapped within the space enclosed by the net, and gradually concentrated towards the centre, or bunt. The foot-rope is hauled in faster than the head-line, so that the fish have less chance to escape. When all the net is up on the beach it is laid out flat, and the fish removed. As our Lord reminds his hearers: the fishermen " store all that is worth keeping in their buckets, and throw the useless kind away ".

Seine or drag-nets were used by the Egyptians, Phoenicians, Greeks and Romans. They are among the most universal of nets and found in almost every part of the world, in one form or another.[1]

6. JESUS CALMS THE WIND AND THE WAVES

Mark 4.35–41 :

That day, when evening came on Jesus said to them, " Let us go across to the other side." So they let the multitude

[1] The Danish seine-net, or *Snurrevaed*, which gradually superseded long and hand-lines in most Scottish fishing districts and also in parts of England after World War I, is merely a modernized version of the seine-net used by Galilean fishermen nineteen hundred years ago. To-day the net is " cast into the sea" from motor vessels fitted with scientific inventions which would have astonished the Apostles, and which they would have regarded as miraculous. It is far easier for the net to " enclose fish of every kind at once ". Special winches and coilers save physical labour in hauling the net. But the fishermen still have to throw " the useless kind away "— the under-sized fish which it is forbidden to land or sell, and which have to be thrown overboard before the vessel reaches port. So there is still " weeping and gnashing of teeth "! Our Lord's parable of the seine-net is repeated daily in countless fishing ports even around our own coasts, and in a more convincing manner than when it was first addressed to his hearers by the Sea of Galilee.

go, and took him with them, just as he was, on the boat. There were other boats too with him.

And a great storm of wind arose, and drove the waves into the boat, so that the boat could hold no more. Meanwhile he was in the stern, asleep on the pillow there.

And they roused him, crying, " Master, art thou unconcerned? We are sinking."

So he rose up, and checked the wind, and said to the sea, " Peace, be still." And the wind dropped, and there was deep calm.

Then he said to them, " Why are you faint-hearted? Have you still no faith?"

And they were overcome with awe. " Why, who is this ", they said to one another, " who is obeyed even by the winds and the sea?"

Matthew 8.24–27:

So he took ship, and his disciples followed him. And suddenly a great storm arose on the sea, so that the waves rose high over the ship; but he lay asleep. And his disciples came and roused him, crying: " Lord, save us, we are sinking." But Jesus said to them: " Why are you faint-hearted, men of little faith?"

Then he rose up, and checked the winds, and the sea, and there was deep calm. So that all asked in amazement: " What kind of man is this, who is obeyed even by the winds and the sea?"

Luke 8.22–25:

A day came when he and his disciples embarked on a boat. " Let us cross to the other side of the lake," he said to them; and they began their voyage. While they were sailing, he fell asleep. And now a storm of wind came down upon the lake, and they began to ship water perilously. So they came and roused him, crying: " Master, master, we are sinking."

And he rose up, and checked both wind and wave, and there was calm. Then he said to them: " Where is your faith? " They were full of awe and astonishment, saying to one another: " Why, who is this, who gives his command to wind and water, and is obeyed? "

Jesus had been preaching all day, teaching the crowds by parables. When evening came he was exhausted, and said to his Apostles: " Let us go across to the other side of the lake." Only on the water could he be certain of obtaining peace, but as it was, " there were other boats too with him ". The people were determined not to let Jesus alone, so they came after him even by sea. The decision to embark appears to have been made in a hurry, for St. Mark says that the disciples took Jesus on the boat " just as he was ". This phrase suggests that they did not bother about taking any food or drink, or even cloaks to keep themselves warm during the night. All that mattered at the moment was to get away from the multitude.

Although Peter, Andrew, James and John had given up fishing as a profession, they must have kept one or more boats for the use of their Master; hence the frequent references in the Gospels to crossing from one side of the lake to the other. Once he was at sea, Jesus could be more or less sure of being unmolested by his importunate followers. He might have said, in the words of Hilaire Belloc, " The sea has taken me to itself whenever I have sought it, and has given me relief from men. It has rendered remote the cares and wastes of the land. . . . The sea shall comfort us, and perpetually show us new things and assure us. It is the common sacrament of the world. May it be to others what it has been to me."[1]

[1] *The Cruise of the Nona,* p. 247.

As the fishermen unloosed the moorings and rowed out from the shore the sun was sinking in the west, its last rays turning the distant mountains to rose-pink and violet, then to grey. A gentle breeze was blowing from off shore. Peter gave orders for the sail to be hauled up. In a few moments it is set taut, and the halyard coiled at the foot of the mast. We may suppose that the nets and gear had been taken off the boat by now as they were no longer needed, so there would have been more space for the disciples and their Master. The other boats, mentioned by St. Mark, were doubtless following this vessel: those on board them were not going to lose sight of the Rabbi, and resolved to be with him wherever he should land on the opposite side of the Lake.

We can picture Peter sitting on the windward side of the boat at the stern, grasping the paddle-shaped tiller in his left hand, with a light but firm touch. With his right hand he loosens the sheet. The boat slips through the water, borne along by the westerly breeze. Jesus has retired to the small decked-in space at the stern. He lies down on a cushion, and is soon fast asleep, his weariness soothed by the gentle lullaby of the water lapping beneath the keel of the boat as she rises and falls on the swell.

Meanwhile Peter keeps an eye to windward, watching the surface of the water and the ravines in the mountain sides, knowing from life-long experience how gusts of wind swoop down them once the sun has set and the upper air begins to cool. The breeze freshens. Dark patches appear on the surface of the water. They grow larger and creep nearer the boat. The crests of the little waves whiten. The boat is now flying before the wind, speeding eastwards.

Peter puts the helm up to ease off the sheet, passing it around a cleat and grasping it more firmly. A sudden squall hits the boat. She heels over. The disciples cling on to the weather side to resist the force of the wind. Peter puts the helm down to bring the boat more on to the wind. The seas start to come over the quarter.

It becomes more difficult to keep the little vessel riding over the white curling crests of the waves, which are following her. There is a danger that she may be pooped. The short choppy seas on this mountain-girt lake can be far more risky than the broad swell of the ocean.

A violent gust strikes the boat, worse than any before. The mast leans at an alarming angle. The gunwale is under water, and the boat begins to fill. She is undecked, except for the stern and the bow. The water is swirling about amidships. The storm rages furiously; the waves rise higher and higher. The men cling to whatever is nearest to their hold. They are terrified that either they will be washed overboard, or the boat will capsize. They grow desperate and lose their nerve. They huddle together for safety. To make themselves heard above the roar of the winds and of the waves and the creaking of the mast and the straining of the sail, they shout: " Master, master, we are sinking! " At last they manage to rouse the sleeper, who seems to be quite unconscious of the danger. Opening his eyes, he rises from his cushion. Gazing out over the raging waters, he bids them be still. The wind drops suddenly. There is a deep calm. The squall has passed.

Turning to the others, he says: " Why are you faint-hearted? Have you still no faith? " As if to remind them that, having the Lord of all creation on board, they should have realized that no harm could befall them. Have they forgotten how God rebuked the Red Sea, and the many passages in the Prophets where the power of God over the sea is stressed? Surely they remember the words of the Psalmist:

They that go down to the sea in ships, doing business in the great waters: these have seen the works of the Lord, and his wonders in the deep.

He said the word, and there arose a storm of wind: and the waves thereof were lifted up.

They mount up to the heavens, and they go down to the depths: their soul pined away with evils.

They were troubled, and reeled like a drunken man: and all their wisdom was swallowed up.

And they cried to the Lord in their affliction: and he brought them out of their distresses.

And he turned the storm into a breeze: and its waves were still.

And they rejoiced because they were still: and he brought them to the haven which they wished for.[1]

What had just taken place was an almost literal fulfilment of this word-picture. And now the Master has "turned the storm into a breeze, and its waves were still". The disciples, sitting around him in their wet clothes, are cold and hungry, for it would appear that they had brought no food with them in their hurried sailing a few hours before. They are overcome with fear and wonder. They whisper to each other: "*Who* can this man be who is obeyed even by the winds and waves?" We can visualize them baling out the water from the boat

[1] Psalm 106, Authorized Version 107.

while she now speeds onward in the darkness of the night, the mountains on the far shore growing nearer and larger as they loom against the eastern sky. We do not know what happened to the other boats. Perhaps they managed to make land or their crews rowed back to where they had set out from before the squall burst.

The first rays of dawn begin to show behind the mountains, and before long the familiar landmarks can be made out—far away to the north-west the white houses of Bethsaida and Capharnaum, pale and ghostly against their background of hills. Further west is Magdala, and more to the south the newly-built palaces and villas of Tiberias catch the first rays of the sun. It would seem that the boat had been driven far out of her course in the storm. The breeze has now dropped, and the fishermen Apostles take to their oars, rowing the boat into a cove " on the further side of the sea, in the country of the Gerasenes ".[1] Here they land, and out rushes to meet them from the rock tombs a naked man, possessed by devils. Jesus heals him, driving the devils into a herd of swine. The pigs rush down a cliff into the Lake and are drowned. A crowd from the surrounding district appear and beg Jesus to leave their country.

Returning to the shore, he boards the boat with his disciples. The man who had been cured wants to go with them, but he is told to seek out his friends and tell them what great mercies had been done to him.

" So Jesus went back by boat across the sea, and a great multitude gathered about him; and while he was still by the sea . . ."[2] This homeward voyage

[1] Mark 5.1.
[2] Mark 5.21.

must have been quieter than that of the previous night, for no details of it are recorded by the Evangelists.

7. THE FEEDING OF THE FIVE THOUSAND

Matthew 14.13–21:

Jesus . . . took ship from the place where he was, and withdrew into desert country, to be alone; but the multitudes from the town heard of it, and followed him there by land. So, when he disembarked, he found a great multitude there, and he took pity on them, and healed those that were sick. And now it was evening, and his disciples came to him and said: " This is a lonely place, and it is past the accustomed hour; give the multitudes leave to go into the villages and buy themselves food there." But Jesus told them: " There is no need for them to go away; it is for you to give them food to eat." They answered: " We have nothing with us, except five loaves and two fishes." " Bring them to me here," he said. Then he told the multitudes to sit down on the grass, and when the five loaves and the two fishes were brought to him, he looked up to heaven, blessed and broke the loaves, and gave them to his disciples; and the disciples gave them to the multitude. All ate and had enough, and when they picked up what was left of the broken pieces they filled twelve baskets with them. About five thousand men had eaten, not reckoning women and children.

Mark 6.41:

. . . dividing the fishes, too, among them all . . . and when they took up the broken pieces, and what was left of the fishes, they filled twelve baskets with them. . . .

See also Luke 9.10–17; John 6.1–14.

Once again Jesus goes on board a boat and " retires across the sea of Galilee ", hoping to escape from the

crowds. Presumably he set sail from Capharnaum
and lands in a secluded bay a few miles along the shore.
Biblical scholars disagree among themselves as to the
location of the hill-side or desert place where the
miracle of the feeding of the five thousand occurred.
Some maintain that it was on the eastern side of the
Jordan, others that it was among the mountains behind
Capharnaum; a valley to the north of the plain of
Genesareth, above the little bay of Ain Tabigah.
However, such differences of topography matter very
little so far as the *maritime* incidents in the story are
concerned. What interests us is that Jesus went by
boat to wherever he landed, and for the purpose of
the subsequent miracle of feeding more than five
thousand persons, he used five barley loaves and
two fishes.

In his narrative of this miracle, St. John uses an
unusual Greek word for fish, *opsarion*, so Edersheim
points out.[1] " It specially refers to the small and
generally dried or pickled fish eaten with bread, like
our ' sardines ', or the ' caviare ' of Russia, the pickled
herrings of Holland and Germany, or a peculiar kind
of small dried fish, eaten with the bones, in the North
of Scotland. Now, just as any one who would name
that fish eaten with bread, would display such minute
knowledge of the habits of the North-east of Scotland
as only personal residence could give, so in regard to
the use of this term, which, be it marked, is *peculiar
to the Fourth Gospel*, Dr. Westcott suggests that ' it may
have been a familiar Galilean word '." The
diminutive form of this word, *opsarion*, derived from
the Greek *opson*, means a " savoury dish ". The
Talmud permitted certain kinds of small fish to be

[1] *Life and Times of Jesus the Messiah*, Vol. I, p. 682.

" They were in the boat . . . repairing their nets " [*Mark 1.19*]

" All the fishes of the sea are delivered into your hand " [*Genesis 9.2*]

eaten raw.   They were supposed to be good for health.
" A kind of pickle or savoury was also made of them."
The Sea of Galilee abounded in such fish.   They were
both salted and pickled for export and home consumption.   So we may picture the five thousand
eating the equivalent of oatcakes and sardines.

It is again worth mentioning that it is the fisherman,
St. John, who uses the word *opseia* (plural) when
describing the fish roasting on the charcoal fire by the
shore in the last chapter of his Gospel.   When Peter
let down the net, he drew it to shore, " full of *great*
fishes ".   But the meal which our Lord invited his
disciples to partake of was still " bread and small
fishes ", even though he had granted them a catch of
large fish.

8.   JESUS AND ST. PETER WALK ON THE SEA OF TIBERIAS

Matthew 14.22-32:

*Jesus prevailed upon his disciples to take ship and cross to
the other side before him, leaving him to send the multitudes
home.   When he had finished sending them home, he went up
by himself on to the hill side, to pray there.*

*Twilight had come, and he remained there alone.   Mean-
while the ship was already half-way across the sea, hard put
to it by the waves, for the wind was against them.*

*When the night had reached its fourth quarter, Jesus came
to them, walking on the sea.*

*When they saw him walking on the sea, the disciples were
terrified.   They said, " It is an apparition ", and cried out
for fear.*

*But all at once Jesus spoke to them, " Take courage ",
he said, " it is myself; do not be afraid."*

*Peter answered him, " Lord, if it is thyself, bid me come
to thee over the water."*

F

He said, " Come ", and Peter let himself down out of the ship, and walked over the water to reach Jesus. Then seeing how strong the wind was, he lost courage and began to sink; whereupon he cried aloud, " Lord, save me." Jesus at once stretched out his hand and caught hold of him, saying to him, " Why didst thou hesitate, man of little faith? "

So they went on board the ship, and thereupon the wind dropped. The ship's crew came and said, falling at his feet, " Thou art indeed the Son of God."

Mark 6.45–52 :

He prevailed upon his disciples to take ship and cross to Bethsaida, on the other side, before him, leaving him to send the multitude home. When he had taken leave of them, he went up on to the hill-side, to pray there. Twilight had already come, and the boat was half way across the sea, while he was on the shore alone. When the night had reached its fourth quarter, seeing them hard put to it with rowing (for the wind was against them), he came to them, walking on the sea, and made as if to pass them by.

When they saw him walking on the sea, they thought it was an apparition, and cried aloud, for all had seen him, and were full of dismay. But now he spoke to them: " Take courage ", he said, " it is myself; do not be afraid."

So he came to them on board the boat, and thereupon the wind dropped. They were astonished out of all measure. They had not grasped the lesson of the loaves, so dulled were their hearts.

John 6.15–21 :

Knowing, then, that they meant to come and carry him off, so as to make a king of him, Jesus once again withdrew on to the hill side all alone. His disciples, when evening came on, went down to the lake and there, embarking on the boat, they began to cross the water to Capharnaum.

Darkness had fallen, and Jesus had not yet come back to them. Meanwhile there was a strong wind blowing, and the sea was beginning to grow rough. Now they had rowed some twenty-five or thirty furlongs, when they saw Jesus walking on the sea, and already drawing near to the boat. They were terrified; but he said to them: " It is myself; do not be afraid." Then they took him on board willingly enough; and all at once their boat reached the land they were making for.

After the vast multitude of men and women had been fed on five barley loaves and two small pickled fish, the people were worked up to such a pitch of emotion that they wanted to proclaim Jesus King of Israel. Even the Apostles might have been swept up by this excitement. Jesus insisted that they were to return to the shore where they had left their boat earlier in the day. When the crowd had dispersed, he retired further into the mountains, meaning to spend the night alone in prayer. He explained that he would meet the Apostles at Bethsaida if they went on by water.

If the boat had been moored on the sandy shore of the little bay of Ain Tabigah, and the feeding of the five thousand had taken place somewhere in what is now known as the Wady el Jamous, " the Valley of Buffaloes ", which opens out into the bay of El Tabigah, then it would have been only a mile or so to row or sail to Bethsaida. On the other hand, if the miracle was performed in a desert place, east of the Jordan, within access of Bethsaida-Julias (as many recent exegetists maintain), then the distance by sea to the supposed site of the other Bethsaida, near Capharnaum, would be about four miles.

The sun set, and a strong wind arose, blowing from the west, or north-west. So, with the sail hoisted, the boat made no progress, and was driven out into the midst of the Lake. The only thing to do, given a wind in this direction, was to take to the oars. We can picture the fishermen-Apostles rowing hard, with the spray breaking over the bow of the boat and beating against their faces. The moon had risen and was shining over the dark waters.

Far away to the north, " Christ is on that hill-top in solitary converse with his Father—praying after that miraculous breaking of bread. . . . Then as he rises from his knees, he looks out over the Lake after that little company, which embodied and represented all that there yet was of his Church, all that would really feed on the Bread from Heaven, and own him their true King. Without presumption, we may venture to say, that there must have been indescribable sorrow and longing in his Heart, as his gaze was bent across the track which the little boat would follow. As we view it, it seems all symbolical: the night, the moonlight, the little boat, the contrary wind, and then also the lonely Saviour after prayer looking across to where the boatmen vainly labour to gain the other shore. As in the clear moonlight just that piece of water stands out, almost like burnished silver, with all else in shadows around, the sail-less mast is now rocking to and fro, without moving forward. They are in difficulty, in danger, and the Saviour cannot pursue his journey on foot by land; he must come to their help, though it be across the water."[1]

It was by now about three hours after midnight. The Apostles were worn out, mentally and physically.

[1] Edersheim, *op. cit.*, Vol. I, p. 691.

After the emotional strain of the afternoon, a reaction was inevitable. The rowers must have been even more exhausted, with the wind against them. They looked aside, and there coming towards the boat was a mysterious figure whom they took to be a ghost, possibly the spirit of a man who had been drowned on the Lake. Terror seized all of them, and they cried out in alarm. At first it seemed as if the figure moving over the tops of the waves was going to pass by the boat. Then the man drew nearer, but still they did not recognize him. When he was in hailing distance and could make himself heard above the roaring of the sea, he called them, saying: " Take courage, it is myself, do not be afraid! " Peter, with his usual impetuosity, answers: " Lord, if it is thyself, bid me come to thee over the water! " The reply is the simple word: " Come! "

Without thinking what he was doing, Peter jumped out of the boat, and started to walk over the choppy sea to reach his Master. Then came a sudden gust of wind, and Peter realized the danger he was in. He began to sink; it is possible, that like many other fishermen, he could not swim. At any rate it would have been difficult to keep afloat in that rough sea. He shouted: " Lord, save me! " By this time he cannot have been far away from Jesus, for the latter stretched out his hand, caught hold of the fisherman; saying: " Why didst thou hesitate, man of little faith? " Hand in hand, the two of them moved towards the boat and climbed aboard. Immediately the wind dropped.

As St. John remarks, the disciples " took him on board willingly enough ". They were overwhelmed at this new miracle which had been performed in the darkness of the night, out on the waters of the Lake. In the words of St. Matthew: " The ship's crew came and said, falling at his feet: ' Thou art indeed the Son of God '." Or as St. Mark puts it: " They were astonished out of all measure. They had not grasped the lesson of the loaves, so dulled were their hearts."

In the previous story of the storm at sea, we are told that there was a great calm; in this incident it is merely stated that the wind dropped. So it is possible that they were able to sail the boat back to Bethsaida from that point " half-way across the sea ", where our Lord had appeared walking on the water. Anyhow, as St. John indicates, it was not long before they " reached the land they were making for ".

The day had dawned by the time they " came to shore at Genesareth and moored there ".[1] Maybe, even before the boat had been tied up, the people who were on the beach noticed her afar off. For we read that " as soon as they had disembarked, Jesus was recognized " by the inhabitants of that place.

NOTE

W. M. Thomson (*The Land and the Book*, ed. 1859, Vol. II, pp. 29 sqq.) has much to say about the storm on the Lake. He is of the opinion that the miracle of the feeding of the five thousand took place at the south-east extremity of Butaiha, a desert place several miles south from where the Jordan runs into the Lake. It would have been a long walk back to the towns on the opposite shore. Jesus had to " prevail " upon his disciples to take ship. They were reluctant to leave him. Probably they hoped to pick him up between the cove where the boat had been moored and Bethsaida, which lay at the mouth of the Jordan (not the other Bethsaida, the fisher-quarter of Capharnaum). Once the wind had sprung up it would have been impossible for the boat to make this Bethsaida;

[1] Mark 6.53.

she would even have been driven past Capharnaum, towards the Plain of Genesareth. "On the supposition that the miracle took place several miles below the mouth of the Jordan, all this is topographically natural. Next day the people found Jesus on the opposite side of the lake."

Thomson records some personal memories of the force of the wind on the Sea of Galilee. "After sunset the wind began to rush down toward the lake, and continued all night with constantly increasing violence, so that when we reached the shore next morning, the face of the lake was like a huge boiling cauldron. The wind howled down every *wady* from the N.E. and E. with such fury that no efforts of rowers could have brought a boat to shore at any point along the coast. In wind like that the disciples *must* have been driven quite across to Genesareth, as we know they were " (p. 32). "These winds are not only violent, but they come down suddenly, and often when the sky is perfectly clear. . . . The faith of Peter in desiring and *daring* to set foot on such a sea is most striking and impressive, even more so, indeed, than its failure after he had made the attempt."

9. PETER GOES FISHING WITH A HOOK AND LINE

Matthew 17.23–26:

When they reached Capharnaum, the collectors of the Temple pence approached Peter, and asked, " Does not your master pay the Temple pence? "

" Yes ", he said.

Soon afterwards he came into the house, and Jesus forestalled him.

" Simon ", he said, " tell us what thou thinkest; on whom do earthly kings impose customs and taxes, on their own sons, or on strangers? "

" On strangers ", Peter told him.

Jesus said to him, " Why then, the children go free. But we will not hurt their consciences; go down to the sea, and cast thy hook; take out the first fish thou drawest up, and when thou hast opened its mouth thou wilt find a silver coin there; with this make payment to them for me and for thyself."

The coasts of Galilee must have swarmed with tax-collectors, for it was a frontier district. There were the local customs-officers, like Matthew, who probably had his office on the quayside at Capharnaum, where he would have watched Jesus coming and going by boat. Among the other detested " publicans " were those who collected the taxes imposed for the upkeep of the Temple at Jerusalem.

One day Peter was stopped by some of these men, who asked if Jesus paid these taxes. Peter answered that he did. Then he returned to his house, where Jesus lodged. The master must have read the thoughts of his fisherman-Apostle, for he immediately put a question to him regarding the payment of taxes by subjects of kings and by strangers dwelling within their dominions. He reminded Peter that the Son of God was not obliged to pay the Temple pence.

It is nowhere related in the Gospels that Peter had gone fishing after his final call to the apostolate, but now Jesus orders him to take a line, go down to the shore, and " cast a hook ". It is probable that Peter still had his nets and lines stowed away in his house: he returned to his old job after he came back to the Sea of Galilee after the Resurrection, for St. John records his remark " I am going out fishing ",[1] and that the other Apostles replied " We, too, will go with thee ".

Jesus had performed a miracle with nets on the occasion of the first great haul of fish; now he would make use of a hook and line—one of the most ancient methods of catching fish, in use long before somebody

[1] John 21.3.

in the remote past had invented a netting needle, to replace the first finger of the left hand, which had hitherto been used to make rough knots in netting. Primitive man had used fish-hooks of chipped flint or bone; then bronze was used, and finally iron. The hook that Jesus told Peter to take down to the Lake was probably a simple pin-shaped instrument. The fisherman did as he was bidden; we can picture him standing on a rock, casting his line, after baiting the hook. The first fish he drew up had a silver coin in its mouth—just what he had been informed would be there. According to one tradition this species of fish was a large eel, known as sheat-fish. H. V. Morton informs us that it was a *musht*, or comb-fish, describing it as " about six inches long, with an enormous head and a comb-like spine that stands up along its back ".[1] This same writer goes on to tell us that " just out of curiosity " he opened the mouth of a comb-fish and placed a ten-piastre piece in it, which coin is the same size as a florin. It went in easily, for the mouth is very large. In its mouth the male *musht* carries about the spawn, and when the young fish grow the mouth of the parent fish " becomes so distended that it is difficult to understand how he can feed himself ".[2]

No doubt Peter carried this fish back to his house, for, since it had scales, it would be regarded as fit for eating. Then he took the silver coin and handed it to the tax-collectors.

10.   THE FEEDING OF THE FOUR THOUSAND

Matthew 15.29-39:

Jesus passed along the sea of Galilee, and went up into a mountain and sat down there. Great multitudes came to

[1] *In the Steps of the Master*, p. 199.   [2] *Ibid.*, p. 200.

him . . . and he healed them. . . . And Jesus asked
his disciples, " How many loaves have you? " They said
" Seven, and a few small fishes ". . . . He took the seven
loaves and the fishes with them, and when he had blessed
and broken he gave these to his disciples, and his disciples
to the multitude. And they all ate and had enough; and
they took up what was left of the broken pieces, seven
hampers full. And so, taking leave of the multitude, he went
on board the ship, and crossed to the region of Magedan.

Mark 8.1-11:

(v. 7) *And they had a few small fishes; these he blessed,*
and ordered that these, too, should be set before them; and
they ate, and had enough. When they picked up what was
left of the broken pieces, it filled seven hampers. About four
thousand had eaten. And so he sent them home. Thereupon
he embarked with his disciples, and went into the part round
Dalmanutha.

Once again we have a miracle of feeding which
takes place within sight of the Sea of Galilee, and in
which a few small fishes were multiplied to satisfy
the hunger of many thousands. From very early
times the place of the feeding of the four thousand
was believed to be on the edge of the mountains
immediately above Tiberias. From here our Lord
came down to the shore and took ship for Magadan
(according to St. Matthew) and Dalmanutha (according to St. Mark). Most authorities agree that
Magadan is merely another name for Magdala, and
that Dalmanutha was either a quarter of that town,
or a neighbouring village. If this opinion is correct,
then, when Jesus " embarked with his disciples "
after reaching the Lake, their voyage could not have
been much longer than two miles.

Here, then, are the chief incidents concerning the apostolate of Christ among the fishermen of the Sea of Galilee. He chose his first four Apostles from this fisher community, when he might just as easily have selected them from any other profession or any other locality. He made his home in their midst when he was driven out of Nazareth. He called Simon, Andrew, James and John to a closer relationship with himself, when they were engaged in fishing or mending their nets. He healed a fisherman's mother-in-law, and performed many other miracles in the fisher quarter of Capharnaum. Again and again he sailed across the inland sea, more often than not to find peace, and to escape from the crowds. One night he calmed a storm at sea, when the boat was in danger of sinking; on another night he walked over the waves, and bade Peter come to him over the water. Twice he fed a vast multitude in a miraculous manner with fish as well as bread. Lastly, he told Peter to cast a hook into the sea, and performed another miracle by placing a coin in its mouth. These are the stories in the Gospels that have a direct reference to the sea, fish, fishing, fishermen, and boats—not very much, perhaps, but no other manner of earning a living is given such prominence by the Evangelists. After the narrative of the Passion, Death and Resurrection of Christ, the Gospel story closes with the return of the fishermen-Apostles to their old job, and the record of a second miraculous draught of fish. So it is true to say that Our Lord's active ministry on earth began with the call of fishermen to be his Apostles, and ends with his farewell to them as they were once again fishing close to the same spot where they have left their nets to follow him.

Chapter IV

THE SEA-COAST OF
TYRE AND SIDON

THE SEA-COAST OF TYRE AND SIDON

A great gathering of the people . . . from the sea coast of Tyre and Sidon—Luke 6.17.

Great crowds followed him . . . and those who lived about Tyre and Sidon—Mark 3.8.

Jesus withdrew into the neighbourhood of Tyre and Sidon—Matthew 15.21; Mark 7.24.

1. CROWDS FROM THE SEA-COAST FOLLOW JESUS

It is a remarkable thing that among the most enthusiastic followers of Jesus should have been the pagan inhabitants of Tyre and Sidon, who for more than two thousand years had been seafarers. We are told by St. Mark and St. Luke that great crowds of them made the forty to sixty mile journey from the coast to listen to his preaching, and to be healed of their bodily and mental diseases. Orthodox Jews regarded the Phoenicians, who were the original inhabitants on this coast, with horror, because they worshipped idols, even Dagon the fish-god. By the time of our Lord, Tyre and Sidon, which had developed into cosmopolitan communities, made up of people from most countries around the Mediterranean, had adopted many religions. The superstitious cults of innumerable deities were practised in these great seaports. But, as is revealed in the story of the healing of the daughter of the Syrophoenician woman, who was a victim of diabolical possession, some of these people had a faith which was far greater than

77

that of the House of Israel.   They realized that they
were outcasts and only fit to feed on the crumbs that
fell from the Master's table, as if they had been dogs.
But their spiritual hunger was so intense, that they
thought nothing of making that journey over the
mountains to the Sea of Galilee.

Before they returned home it may be supposed that
they begged Jesus to visit their coastal towns and
villages, telling him that there were hundreds of
others who were waiting to hear his message and
needing a physician to cure their diseases.   Sooner or
later, so it is stated by St. Matthew and St. Mark,
" Jesus withdrew into the neighbourhood of Tyre and
Sidon ".

2.   TYRE

Once known as " The Queen of the Seas ", and
one of the greatest and richest ports on the Mediterranean, Tyre to-day is no more than a small and
rather shabby little town.   The prophecy of Ezechiel
has been fulfilled: " They shall break down the walls
of Tyre and destroy the towers thereof: and I will
scrape her dust from her and make her like a smooth
rock.   She shall be a drying place for nets in the
midst of the sea."[1]   A few fishing boats, with their
picturesque lateen sails, and other small craft are
moored in the old harbour.   Nets are spread over
the ruins of ancient monuments.   The sea-trade is
insignificant.

Two thousand years ago, Tyre must have been
very much the same kind of seaport as are Liverpool,
Marseilles, Rotterdam, Antwerp or Buenos Aires
to-day.   Such was the world into which our Lord
brought his disciples.   They would have found a

[1] Ezechiel 26.4–5.

city full of splendid buildings with signs of vast wealth
and corruption on every side.   The Phoenicians had
founded the city about two thousand years before Christ.

When Egypt began to decline about 1300 B.C., the
Phoenicians succeeded to their maritime supremacy
and retained it for many centuries.   They were an
amphibious race, from necessity as well as by choice.
Their country was so small that, like the Dutch or
the English in later centuries, they depended on the
sea for their growth and expansion.   " Tyre and
Sidon were the first ports of the western world from
which a land nation put forth to sea for trade and
conquest.   No one before the Phoenicians had ever
founded a real colony such as Tripoli or Carthage,
and no one before them had an armed navy.
Independently of the Egyptians, they discovered
navigation, astronomy, and arithmetic; they invented
glass, fine linen fabrics, purple dye, and even a better
form of alphabet.   They gathered wares from all the
world, the silver of Tarshish, the gold of Thasos, the
incense of Arabia, and ivory of India."[1]

The disciples, as they gazed at the vessels in the
harbour, must have recalled how King Solomon
engaged Tyrian sailors to float cedar to Joppa for the
building of the temple at Jerusalem.   Tyre had risen
again after Alexander the Great had captured the
city in 322 B.C.   It had passed into the hands of the
Seleucids, and in 65 B.C. the Romans had taken
possession of it, designating it a Free Port.   Herod
built a great temple and laid out squares and fine
public buildings.

The city covered a vast area.   The older portion
had been built on a rocky island.   Other islands were

[1] Emil Ludwig, *The Mediterranean*, p. 59.

G

eventually linked up with it by causeways, and the houses spread over the plain on the mainland. There were two harbours; the one to the north, the other to the south, each protected by breakwaters. Peter, Andrew, James and John would have noticed very different types of craft from those with which they were familiar on their inland sea. The fishing boats were larger and there were cargo vessels, which depended entirely on sail-power. Their rigging must have interested the fishermen-Apostles, as well as the stern-posts projecting upwards into the head of a swan or other bird. Some of these merchant ships were able to carry from 120 to 200 tons of stores apiece. It would have been worth while to have overheard what Peter had to say about the *artemon* or bowsprit which projected over the bow. By that date this feature was found in most Roman merchantmen. In addition to the mainsail on the vertical mainmast and the spritsail on the *artemon*, some of these vessels set two triangular topsails above the mainyard. Most likely this visit to Tyre was the first contact the fisher-men-Apostles would have had with any ships other than those on the Lake of Tiberias. It may have been their first sight of the sea; the first time they had looked across a stretch of water which ended in a flat horizon instead of mountains. Had they any inkling that, a few years later, they would be boarding these Roman merchantmen as passengers and making long voyages at a great distance from land?

Then there were the warships, with their projecting platforms at the bow and stern; their poops covered with awnings to afford shelter from the sun and rain. Some of these had many oars besides their great single square sails. Slaves worked the oars. Lastly, Peter and the other fishermen may have wondered at the size and build of the grain-ships, if, by chance, one or two of these mighty vessels happened to have been driven out of their normal course from Alexandria to Italy by contrary winds. The Galilean fishing boats were mere cockle-shells beside the corn-ships, many of which were nearly 100 feet long.

Perhaps the Apostles, when they looked at all these craft, may have remembered the picture of Tyre drawn by the prophet Ezechiel. He had described the downfall of the port, how the men of war and their crews would " fall in the heart of the sea in the day of the ruin of Tyre; how the fleet would be troubled at the sound of the cry of the pilots ", and how " all that handled the oar shall come down from their ships; the mariners and all the pilots of the sea shall stand on land ".[1]

Such had been the fate of this great port, so they were aware; but there was little evidence of it three centuries later. The Galilean fishermen, when they got home, would have no difficulty in describing the city (in the words of Ezechiel) as " the mart of the people of many islands, set in the heart of the sea: a place of perfect beauty ".[2] There were still great ships planked with boards of fir trees from Mount Hermon, with masts made of the trunks of the tall cedars of Lebanon. The oak forests of Bashan still provided wood for the oars. Had they gone on board some of the merchantmen, they would have found cabins filled with precious objects from Cyprus and the Grecian Isles. Those sails flapping in the breeze were made from Egyptian linen. The gaily coloured awnings were embroidered with scarlet and purple

[1] Ezechiel 27.28, 29.   [2] 27.3.

from the islands of Elisa.   Arabian oarsmen made up
the crews of some of the galleys.   Wherever they went
in the streets round the harbours they met seamen
from Tyre itself and from other places on the coast.[1]

In other ways the port had changed very little from
the description given by Ezechiel, at least in the broad
outline.   There was still the same jostling crowd of
merchants and traders from all parts of the world.
The Carthaginians sold silver, iron, tin and lead.   The
Greeks imported brass vessels, and supplied slave
labour.   There were Armenian horse-dealers, black-
skinned Ethiopians, selling ivory and ebony.   In the
streets were groups of slaves from Asia Minor.   The
bazaars and fairs were full of Syrians who did business
in precious stones, embroidery, silks and linen.   Piled
up on the quays were casks of wine from over the
mountains, and bales of wool, waiting to be put aboard
the cargo ships.   Arabs from as far off as the Persian
Gulf wandered about the fairs, trying to find buyers
for iron, cassia and calamus. Merchants from Southern
Arabia were selling carpets and tapestries.   Flocks of
sheep and goats held up the traffic in the streets.
There were " beauty shops ", patronized by the
women of Tyre, which sold scents, spices, powder and
paint from Sheba and Raamah.   Caravans arrived
from the far distant banks of the Tigris and Euphrates,
with heavy chests, made of cedar wood and bound
with cords, also bales of cloth and embroidered fabrics.
Such wealth and luxury were never seen on such a
scale in any of the fishing ports of Galilee, even if
they were comparatively rich.

Tyre would have been unique among great seaports
of any age or country if it lacked certain streets which

[1] Cf. Ezechiel 27.

catered for the amusement of seafarers.   Doubtless it
possessed the Phoenician equivalent of the S. Pauli
quarter at Hamburg, the Schiedamsche Dijk at
Rotterdam, or narrow alleys that used to lead off the
" Vieux Port " at Marseilles.   As saints are often
found in close proximity with sinners, it is more than
likely that many of the crowds who flocked to Galilee
to hear the preaching of Jesus may have been drawn
from such a quarter of Tyre.   Our Lord was alive
to the wickedness and vices of this port, but he pro-
claimed, later on, if it had witnessed the miracles done
in the fishing ports beside the Lake of Tiberias, the
people would have repented in sackcloth and ashes.

We do not know how long our Lord and his
disciples remained in Tyre, but even if their visit
lasted only a few days, it must have been a revelation
of a greater world to his companions.   He had shown
them the sea and the ships in which they would take
passage in a few years from that date.   He had
introduced them to the cosmopolitan maritime environment of a typical seaport.   The impression left on the
minds of the four fishermen, Peter, Andrew, James
and John, must have been very similar to that which
would be left if fishermen from the coast of Brittany
were taken to visit Le Havre, or a similar group of
fishermen from the Moray Firth ports in Scotland
were conducted around the docks of Glasgow, or four
German fisherlads from the Frisian Islands shown the
sights of Hamburg before this great Free Port was
laid waste during the Second World War.

3.   THE SEA-COAST OF TYRE AND SIDON

The greater part of the twenty-five mile coast line
between Tyre and Sidon consists of sandy beaches or

rocky coves. Behind them the land rises up to the
mountains, with not much level ground behind the
sea, except in a few places where the slopes are broken
by small rivers or streams. The Phoenicians looked
to the sea rather than to the land as a means
of acquiring wealth. Wherever there was a sandy
beach upon which to draw up their boats or ships, or
a sheltered cove where they could ride at anchor, a
village sprang up. Jesus and his disciples would have
taken the same road along the coast as does the modern
traveller. Yet two thousand years ago the scene must
have been very different from what it is to-day.
The almost tideless sea would still have been crashing
against the rocks, or washing the sand and shingle,
but instead of desolation, ruins and a few poor farms,
there would have been villages and towns full of
maritime life. The sounds of shipbuilding, the
whirring of saws, the harsh blows of axe and adze,
the smell of pitch, paint and timber, and all the many
other sounds and smells found in any port—all these
would have claimed their notice. Gathered around
the vessels would have been the bronzed seamen, who
could spin many a yarn of long voyages from one end
of the Mediterranean to the other. Some may have
even pushed westwards through the Straits of Gibraltar
to the Canary Islands, have crossed the Bay of Biscay,
even to Britain. Others would boast how their
ancestors had circumnavigated Africa five hundred
years earlier. Along this coast in the time of our
Lord there would have been Roman garrisons to keep
watch over the native inhabitants.

As Jesus and his disciples moved north along the
coast road after leaving Tyre, they would have noticed
men collecting shell-fish which had been driven up on

to the sand. After a storm they could be found in vast quantities. But this species of fish—*murex brandaris* or *conchylium*—was not used as food: the fragile shells were ground in mills. The juice of the flesh produced the world-famous Tyrian Purple. There were two shades; a light scarlet and a dark crimson. The latter was much the same tint as what is now known as "Roman Purple", and became a symbol of royalty. These tiny shell-fish had been one of the chief sources of wealth to the Phoenicians for thousands of years. The scarlet cloak which the soldiers put on Jesus after they had scourged him had been dyed in the juices of the crushed shell-fish gathered on the sea-coast of Tyre and Sidon.

On their left were the sandy beaches, broken by low headlands, with the white surf breaking over the rocks. With a never-ending monotony, the waves chased towards the shore; hesitating, swelling up, and toppling over with a heavy fall. In quivering beds of foam the waters swelled up over the beach.[1]

So they moved on mile after mile. No doubt they met some of those who had come from this coast to listen to our Lord's preaching. They passed through the port of Ornithopolis, the ruins of which are strewn along the sea about ten miles north of Tyre. Then the party came to another port, Sarepta, situated on a rocky promontory, with a natural harbour among the rocks. It was here, according to tradition, that Jesus cured the daughter of the Syrophoenician woman who was "troubled by an evil spirit".[2] Following the sea all the way, through other towns and villages inhabited mainly by seafarers, they reached Sidon.

[1] Cf. Thomson, *The Land and the Book*, Vol. II, p. 124.
[2] Matthew 15.21–29.

4.　SIDON

Here was another great city which owed its importance to maritime power. It was older even than Tyre. At the present time Sidon has not fallen quite so low as Tyre. Until recent years the port carried on a fairly busy trade in exporting fruit, tobacco, cotton and olive oil. Nature had provided Sidon with two harbours, thanks to rocks that spread out from the shore. The Sidonians were famous as sailors and merchants for more than two thousand years before Christ. They had founded colonies in Cyprus, the Grecian Isles, in Libya and in Spain. Like Tyre, the city of Sidon had a checkered history. It was conquered in turn by the Egyptians, the Assyrians, the Greeks and the Romans. Again and again Sidon rose from its ruins and regained its prosperity. Under the Romans it became a very important centre; Herod the Great built a theatre, and the city had its senate.

The fishermen-Apostles would have found the same type of ships in the harbours as in Tyre. Just as to-day, the waves would have been breaking against the rocks, and if there was a storm, crashing over the houses and flooding the quays. If by chance they had arrived in Sidon in the early spring, all along the shore outside the town, the local cargo vessels would be drawn up, waiting to be launched. Ship-wrights would have been at work, caulking their seams with pitch, repainting them, and reconditioning the vessels for their long voyages across the Mediterranean, even to far distant Spain or Morocco. Laden with merchandise these ships traded with foreign countries throughout the summer; for, as we read in the fifteenth book of the Odyssey of Homer,

> " A ship of Sidon anchored in our port,
> Freighted with toys of every sort—
> With gold and amber chains,
> Each female eye the glittering links employ;
> They turn, review, and cheapen every toy."

In the streets and bazaars they would have mingled with the same cosmopolitan crowds of merchants, peddlers and hawkers as at Tyre.

So, having stayed awhile on shores of the Mediterranean, Jesus and his disciples returned to the Sea of Galilee. It was, so we may presume, their first experience of " dock-walloping " outside the fishing ports of their home-land. " The lure of dockland ", as we are reminded by Miss C. Fox Smith, " is akin to, yet subtly different from, the charm of the sea. The latter is, in a sense, impersonal, almost abstract: the former is bound up with the human aspect— with ships and the men who sail in them, who are, moreover, in continual warfare with the very element they live by. It has the fascination and romance which belong to hard, perilous, wandering lives. It appeals to most of the simple, natural instincts—wonder, curiosity, adventure—which are a part of the equipment of most healthy human beings."[1] Can we doubt if the four fishermen-Apostles, who were very healthy human beings, with simple natural instincts, would not have been interested in the maritime life of Tyre and Sidon and failed to be lured by their " dockland "?

The world in which they found themselves was much the same as in any other port of our own day, for " dockland, strictly speaking, is of no country, or rather of all countries ". Tyre and Sidon, like every other great port, had their " Sailor Towns ", inhabited

[1] *Sailor Town Days*, p. 4.

by an ever shifting, changing population ; an amphibious country on which the sea has set its mark. Peter, Andrew, James and John would have smelt the unvaried smells of ropes and canvas, tar and paint. Wandering through the narrow streets they would have found the shops which in one way or other make a living out of the seafaring community; the bars, saloons and cafés; the junk-stores, full of goods, old and new, brought from every corner of the world.

As they watched those sturdy little merchantmen, hoisting sail, and catching the breeze as they passed out of the harbour on to the deep blue Mediterranean flecked with white horses, perhaps over the swell resounded the words of the local version of a more modern sea-chanty:

" Bound away—bound away—where the wild
                                    waters flow—
She's a packet of Sidon—oh, Lord, let her go! "

Chapter V

THE FISHERMEN-APOSTLES GO BACK TO THEIR NETS AFTER THE RESURRECTION

THE FISHERMEN-APOSTLES GO BACK TO THEIR NETS AFTER THE RESURRECTION

Go and tell Peter and the rest of his disciples that he is going before you into Galilee—Mark 16.7.

Simon Peter told them, " I am going out fishing "; and they said: " We, too, will go with thee." So they went out and embarked on the boat—John 21.3.

THE fishermen-Apostles lost touch with the sea for the greater part of the last year of Christ's active ministry. Their journeys were mostly undertaken overland and not on the waters of the Lake of Tiberias. They were privileged to share in some of the most important events in the life of our Lord. It was to Peter the fisherman that he handed over the keys of the kingdom of heaven, stating that Peter would be the rock upon which his Church would be built.[1] Three of the four fishermen were the only witnesses of the Transfiguration.[2] It was the fishermen-brothers, James and John, the Sons of Thunder, who asked their Master to order fire to come down from heaven to consume the inhabitants of the Samaritan village.[3] Their mother, Salome, begged Jesus to grant them a special place in his kingdom, that they might sit on his right hand and on his left. But all he promised was that they should drink of his cup, that is share in

[1] Matthew 16.13–20.
[2] Matthew 17.1–8; Mark 9.2–8; Luke 9.28–36.
[3] Luke 9.54–56.

his sufferings in years to come. We get a whiff of the sea when Jesus refers to the salt which has lost its savour,[1] but no more. Peter takes a prominent place throughout the story of the Passion, in every incident behaving with his characteristic impetuosity, not only when he cut off the ear of the servant of the High Priest,[2] but when he insisted that the whole body must be washed as well as his feet.[3] Both he and the other fishermen fell asleep in the Garden of Gethsemani when our Lord was in his agony.[4] They could keep awake when fishing at night, but not in this moment of crisis. Lastly, it was Peter the fisherman who was the only Apostle who deliberately denied his Master; but his Galilean dialect gave him away, when he swore with an oath: " I know nothing of this man."[5]

There is a tradition, so H. V. Morton informs us,[6] that Zebedee, the father of James and John, was not only a fisherman, but also a fish merchant, with a branch office in Jerusalem, from which the family of Caiaphas, the High Priest, used to buy their fish. This fact, if it is true, might account for St. John being known to the door-keeper, and thus being able to bring St. Peter in to the court of the High Priest,[7] when otherwise the Galilean fisherman would have had to remain outside. Perhaps St. John used to go around to the back door and deliver the fish, when he was working at his father's shop in Jerusalem.

[1] Luke 14.34.
[2] Matthew 26.51; Mark 14.47; Luke 22.50; John 18.10.
[3] John 13.1–17.
[4] Matthew 26; Mark 14.37–41; Luke 22.43–46.
[5] Matthew 26.69–75 ; Mark 14.66–72 ; Luke 22.54–62 ; John 18.17–27.
[6] *In the Steps of the Master*, p. 219.
[7] John 18.16.

It was Peter and John who ran to the tomb, when Mary Magdalen told them that it was empty. " They began running side by side, but the other disciple outran Peter, and reached the tomb first."[1] Our Lord first appeared to Peter after the Resurrection.[2]

Then the Apostles made their way back to Galilee, for Jesus had told them that he would precede them and would meet them there.[3]

THE RISEN CHRIST APPEARS ON THE SHORES
OF GALILEE

John 21.1–13:

Jesus appeared to his disciples again afterwards, at the sea of Tiberias, and this is how he appeared to them. Simon Peter was there, and with him were Thomas, who is also called Didymus, and Nathanael, from Cana of Galilee, and the sons of Zebedee, and two more of the disciples. Simon Peter told them: " I am going out fishing "; and they said, " We, too, will go with thee."

So they went out and embarked on the boat; and all that night they caught nothing. But when morning came, there was Jesus standing on the shore; only the disciples did not know that it was Jesus.

" Have you caught anything, friends? " Jesus asked them, " to season your bread with? " And when they answered " No ", he said to them: " Cast to the right of the boat, and you will have a catch."

So they cast the net, and found before long they had no strength left to haul it in, such a shoal of fish was in it. Whereupon the disciple whom Jesus loved said to Peter: " It is the Lord." And Simon Peter, hearing him say that it was the Lord, girded up the fisherman's coat which was

[1] John 20.3–4; Luke 24.12.
[2] Luke 24.34.
[3] Matthew 28.10; Mark 16.7.

*all he wore, and sprang into the sea. The other disciples
followed in the boat (they were not far from land, only some
hundred yards away), dragging their catch in the net
behind them.*

*So they went ashore, and found a charcoal fire made there,
with fish and bread cooking on it.*

*" Bring some of the fish you have just caught ", Jesus
said to them.*

*Simon Peter, going on board, hauled in the net to land.
It was loaded with great fish, a hundred and fifty-three of
them; and with all that number the net had not broken.*

*When Jesus said to them: " Come and break your fast ",
none of the disciples ventured to ask him: " Who art
thou? " knowing well that it was the Lord. So Jesus came
up and took bread, which he gave to them, and fish as well.*

The Gospel written by a fisherman records the
story of the calling of the first three fishermen-Apostles
in its opening chapter, and ends with the story of a
miraculous draught of fish. The funds of the community had been lost when Judas betrayed his Master,
so the obvious thing to do was for the fishermen-
Apostles to resume their former occupation. On their
return to the Sea of Galilee, Peter took down his nets
from the store, looked them over and mended them,
and told the other three that he was going to start
fishing. They decided that they would follow his
example. Presumably the rest, having lost their jobs,
felt they might as well make up a crew. Somehow
they had to earn a living to support themselves and
their families. No doubt the boat needed overhauling,
tarring and painting. Maybe the sail had to be
patched, and new ropes bought for the nets. All this
would cost money.

" Stand out into the deep water, and let down your nets for a catch " [*Luke 5·4*]

" . . . For they were fishermen " [*Matthew 4.18; Mark 1.16*]

When the boat was ready for sea, and the nets put
on board, they set out one evening from the shore,
just as so often in the past. The men shot and hauled
their nets all night, but had no luck. They caught
nothing. So "when morning came" they rowed
into one of the little bays, where they would tie up the
boat before going home. We can picture the Lake,
cold and grey and unruffled, with a pink glow behind
the mountains of Gergesa on the opposite shore dim
and mysterious. Higher and higher the light rises;
the air grows warmer, the sea turning from grey-green
to blue, as at last the sun itself comes over the mountain
range.

The fishermen are sitting in their boat, most likely
mending their nets, or possibly merely discussing the
reasons for having taken no fish, or arguing, in the
way that all fishermen do, as to where they should
shoot their nets, or the reasons why the shoals had
disappeared from the usual places.

At that hour of the morning they would not
have been in the best of tempers. The one man may have
been blaming the other, even hinting that there had
been a Jonah on board. It is certain that the muscles
of their backs and arms had grown slack from lack
of practice at rowing, or any other form of hard
labour for a year or more. Their hands would be
soft, and doubtless blisters had arisen when they were
toiling at the heavy oars. Anybody who has not done
any rowing for a long time will understand these
details.

They glance up towards the beach and notice a
man walking in their direction. He is a stranger, and
they do not recognize him. He comes nearer, and
when he is close to the boat, he hails them saying:

H

" Have you caught anything, friends, to season your bread with? " The crew answer that they have no fish on board.

The stranger then tells them to cast their net on the starboard side of the boat, and if they do this, they will be lucky. What was their immediate reaction to this command we do not know; did they remember how they had been given the same order by Jesus in the past, and on that occasion two boats had been filled with fish? Anyhow, they cast their net, and in a few moments it was so heavy that they could not haul it in. John—the fisherman who tells the story— relates that he turned to Peter, saying: " It is the Lord ", and goes on to record how the ever-impetuous Peter, girded up his " fisherman's coat ", and jumped into the water.

The Galilean fishermen worked with their limbs bare, except often for a linen cloth, girt about their loins, reaching half way down to their thighs. The point to be noticed here is that, out of respect for his Master, Peter put on his coat, whether he was wearing a loin-cloth or was completely naked. Presumably he tucked his coat into his belt before he leapt off the boat, and splashed through the shallow water in his eagerness to reach the shore. The rest of the crew took their oars and rowed in towards the beach: St. John tells us that " they were not far from land, only some hundred yards away ". The net was dragged behind the boat.

When the men got ashore, they found a charcoal fire had been lit. But where had the fish and bread come from that were being baked over the embers?

Jesus tells them to bring some of the fish which they had taken. Peter went back on board, hauled the net on to the beach and took out the fish.   St. John uses a Greek word that indicates that they were large fish—not small fish such as were being cooked on the fire.   The total catch was one hundred and fifty-three. " Who but a fisherman, or one intimately acquainted with them, would dream of making the amazingly matter-of-fact statement at such a moment that ' with all that number the net had not broken '? "[1]

Breakfast is now ready. Jesus bids the fishermen gather around the fire, knowing that they must be hungry. He hands them the freshly baked bread and divides among them the small fish. As they sat there on the shore, none of them dared to ask if this man were really Jesus, although they knew in their hearts he was their Master who had risen from the dead, and who, as he had foretold, had gone before them into Galilee.

When the meal was ended, Jesus turned to Peter, saying: " Dost thou care for me more than these others? " Peter answered: " Yes, Lord, thou knowest well that I love thee! "   Three times this same question was asked, and the same reply given. Finally, the fisherman who had denied that he had ever met Jesus, exclaimed passionately: " Lord, thou knowest all things; thou canst tell that I love thee! "

Then came the orders that Peter was to stop catching any more fish, and devote himself to feeding the lambs, yearlings and the full-grown sheep. What did he make of such an odd command? What would any fisherman feel if he were " directed " (in the modern sense) to work on the land, to become a farm-servant? Granted that our Lord was using the words symbolically, yet one ventures to think that Peter's

[1] H. V. Morton, *In the Steps of the Master*, p. 199.

response might have been more wholehearted if his Master had used the imagery of the sea instead of the land. However, by doing so it merely stressed the fact that from now onwards Peter would not be a free agent: another would bind him, and he would not be able to escape from the yoke of Christ.

By this time it seems that Jesus and Peter had moved away from the others. Peter turned around and saw the other fisherman, John, following them. " What of this man? What is going to happen to him? " he asks. It was this fisherman, more than all the other disciples to whom Jesus had always shown a particular affection. His answer to Peter's question is difficult to understand: it might have several meanings. But some of those who heard those words believed that the Beloved Disciple would never see death. " It's none of your business! " Jesus said in so many words: " Your job, from now onwards, is to follow me, wherever I shall send you . . . you turned your back and denied me in the past. Never do so again."

The fisherman who bore witness of this event assures us that it is true. If he had recorded everything else that he remembered about those three years he spent with his Master, the world itself would not contain the books which would have to be written.

Chapter VI

THE FISHERMEN TAKE SHIP TO
FAR DISTANT COUNTRIES

Chapter VI

THE FISHERMEN TAKE SHIP TO
FAR DISTANT COUNTRIES

I will make you into fishers of men—Matthew 4.19.

Stand out into the deep water—Luke 5.4.

Go out all over the world and preach the gospel to the whole of creation—Mark 16.15.

THE missionary journeys of the Apostles would have been even more difficult had it not been for the extension of the Roman Empire right round the Mediterranean. Thirty years before Christ, Augustus, after the Battle of Actium, had succeeded in stamping out piracy, enforcing maritime peace and maritime order. For the first time in history the Mediterranean was made safe for trade. The early Christians had no difficulty in finding ships which called at the ports they wished to visit on their apostolic journeys. It is probably true to state that maritime communications on the Mediterranean were easier two thousand years ago than they are to-day. The ships were much smaller; they depended on the winds for progression and sailed only between March and September, except in rare circumstances. Nevertheless sea-travel was infinitely less complicated, and there was no bother about passports or currency regulations. It was easier for the Apostles to obey our Lord's command: " Go out, and make disciples of all nations ", than it would be if he had delivered this same order at the present time. Rome had made the

Here he was crucified, bound to the cross by his wrists and ankles. His relics were taken to Amalfi, on the peninsula of Sorrento, where they are still enshrined in the cathedral of this little city, largely inhabited by fishermen.

The voyages of James the fisherman are even more legendary. He is supposed to have sailed from Palestine to Spain, where he engaged in missionary work. All we know for certain is that he was put to death in his own country by the order of Herod.

His brother, John, must have been quite familiar with the Mediterranean. From Ephesus he was banished to the rocky island of Patmos, in the midst of the Aegean. It is possible that before this exile he had been in Italy, for according to Tertullian he had been cast into a cauldron of boiling oil at Rome. From Patmos, John was able to return to Ephesus after the death of the Emperor Domitian. The aged fisherman spent his last years in this port of Asia Minor.

Of the voyages of Philip, who, like the fishermen-Apostles, was a native of Bethsaida, nothing authentic has been recorded. All we gather is that he travelled around Asia Minor. Eusebius mentions that Bartholomew made his way to India, but this word then covered a very wide area and may have meant nothing farther afield than Arabia. Other legends suggest that Bartholomew may have sailed across the Mediterranean to Egypt, and even voyaged on the Black Sea.

The apocryphal documents concerning the Apostle, Thomas, the authenticity of which is extremely doubtful, relate that he sailed to India. Some versions of these legends make him go as far east as Pekin in China. Believe it or not, the Apostle is said to have preached the Gospel on the island of Socotra, and then sailed over to the western coast of India. However, the verdict of Dr. Adrian Fortescue is that " the apostolic origin of Malabar Christianity is a very doubtful legend ".[1]

The long missionary journeys of Matthew, the publican, appear to have been made by land. James the Less does not seem to have moved out of Palestine. Thaddeus, otherwise known as Jude, also confined his apostolate to the land and made no voyages on any sea.

ST. PETER AT JOPPA

One of the most outstanding events in the life of Peter the fisherman took place at Joppa—the revelation that all men are equal in the sight of God. He was granted this inward vision when gazing across the Mediterranean from the roof of the house of Simon, the tanner, where he was lodging. The house was close to the sea, as is mentioned by St. Luke.[2] The traditional site is still pointed out. The present house, which has an outside stair and a flat roof, must be very similar to the one in which Peter stayed. About half a century ago, workmen discovered several tanners' vats within a few yards of the house, when an ancient sea wall was being demolished.[3]

" We can understand that as Peter moved about the narrow lanes of Joppa, leading to the sea, where his scrupulous countrymen were jostled by foreign sailors and foreign wares, he grew more concerned than ever about the ceremonial law."[4]   He would have studied

---

[1] *The Lesser Eastern Churches*, p. 356.
[2] Acts 10.6.
[3] Joppa—the modern Jaffa—is now a busy city with a population of over 100,000. In 1936 a new harbour was built at the north end of the port to serve the Jewish city of Tel Aviv. It is the seaport for Jerusalem.
[4] G. A. Smith, *op. cit.*, p. 141.

the ships in the harbour as a professional seaman. He would have talked to the sailors from many countries around the Mediterranean. Then, as now, there would have been stevedores and dock labourers, carrying enormous loads of merchandise on their backs, for the streets leading from the quays into the town are far too narrow for carts. The burdens imposed by the Pharisees were even heavier than the bales shouldered by these workmen. Whenever Peter cast his eyes over the sea, he would have been reminded of those invisible islands and far distant countries with which the ships traded. He realized that the world was much bigger than that in which he had been brought up on and around the Lake of Tiberias.

One morning, when waiting for his dinner, he climbed up to the roof of Simon's house, with its pungent smell of leather. Far away to the east were the distant hills of Judea, lost in a haze. Below him was the small harbour, crowded with ships of many nations; some with their square sheet-like mainsail furled, others with them flapping in the breeze. To the west he gazed over the blue waters of the Mediterranean, sparkling in the blinding glare of the midday sun.

The fisherman was hungry, so St. Luke remarks, and Simon's wife was keeping him waiting for dinner. It was very hot up on the roof. As he prayed, he " fell into a trance ", or he may have just dropped asleep. In his dream " he saw heaven opening, and a bundle, like a great sheet, let down by its four corners on to the earth; in it were all kinds of four-footed beasts, and things that creep on the earth, and all the birds of heaven. And a voice came to him, saying: ' Rise up, Peter, lay about and eat! ' Peter answered: ' It cannot be, Lord; never in my life have I eaten anything profane, anything unclean.' Then the voice came to him a second time: ' It is not for thee to call anything profane, which God has made clean.' Three times this happened, and then the bundle was drawn up again into heaven."[1]

Was this " great sheet " merely an inward recollection of one of those four-cornered square sails, laid out on the ground? It would have looked like a bundle before it was unloosed.

Peter awoke from his dream, and while he was " turning over the vision in his mind ", he was made aware that three men were waiting for him down below. He discovered that they had come from the centurion, Cornelius, who wanted him to go to the port of Caesarea to instruct him in the Faith.

The three messengers spent the night in Joppa, and the following morning Peter accompanied them on the thirty mile journey northward along the coast to Caesarea. There the centurion and his closest friends and relatives were awaiting the party. It was in this port that Peter explained, for the first time, that now he saw clearly " that God makes no distinction between man and man; that he welcomes anybody, whatever his race, who fears him and does what piety demands ".[2] It was in the house of the Roman centurion that the first Gentile Pentecost took place, and where the fisherman baptized all those who had listened to his preaching, and who had received the Holy Ghost, " just as we did ".

Twenty-five years before Christ, Herod the Great had transformed the tiny bay of the little pagan town

[1] Acts 10.9–17.
[2] Acts 10.35.

called the Tower of Straton into a seaport. Within
twelve years he had built a great city, which he named
Caesarea, in honour of Caesar Augustus. The ancient
port of Joppa remained intensely Jewish, and declined.
Caesarea became more and more important; Roman
in obedience, Greek in culture. The harbour was
protected by a vast breakwater, 200 feet wide.
Josephus tells us that it was fortified, and that there
were a great number of arches, where the sailors lodged,
and a long quay, which " was a most pleasant walk
for such as had a mind for exercise ". The entrance
was at the north " on which side was the gentlest of
all the winds in this place ". It was the only real
harbour on the coast. For many years this great port
was the virtual capital of Palestine.[1] It was from
Caesarea that St. Paul sailed on his last missionary
voyage, and where he landed from Ephesus. To-day
this great city and its harbour lie in ruins.

[1] See G. A. Smith, *op. cit.*, pp. 139–140.

Chapter VII

THE VOYAGES OF ST. PAUL

Chapter VII

THE VOYAGES OF ST. PAUL

What journeys I have undertaken . . . in danger in the sea!—II Cor. 11.26.

I have been shipwrecked three times—II Cor. 11.25.

I. ST. LUKE AND THE SEA

Luke, the physician and fellow-labourer with Paul, must have had a wonderfully retentive memory in addition to powers of observation. What is also remarkable is his knowledge of nautical matters. This proves that he must have spent much of his life at sea, but not as a seaman, "for his language, although accurate, is not professional".[1] W. M. Ramsay[2] maintains that Luke " has the Greek feeling for the sea, a feeling that must develop in every race possessing any capacity for development, and any sensitiveness to the influence of nature when settled round the Aegean coast, with its regular winds and regular sunset calm, when the water lies dead, with a surface which looks like oil, dense and glistening and dark that it seems to invite one to walk upon it ". This same authority points out that " everyone who compares Luke's account of the journey from Caesarea to Jerusalem (which might be expected to live in his memory beyond others), or from Puteoli to Rome, with his account of any of the voyages, must be struck by the difference between the scanty matter of details

[1] James Smith, *The Voyage and Shipwreck of St. Paul*, p. 21.
[2] *St. Paul, the Traveller and Roman Citizen*, p. 205.

in the land journeys, and the love that notes the voyage, the winds, the runs, the appearance of the shores, Cyprus rising out of the sea, the Cretan coast close in by the ship's side, the mountains towering above it from which the blast strikes down. . . . His interest in the sea sprang from his natural and national character, and not from his occupation ".[1]

James Smith[2] notices that when Luke describes nautical incidents, " he tells us what has happened, but rarely tells us how or why the measures connected with it were taken. In doing so he often mentions circumstances which a seaman would not think of noticing from their familiarity, or from being taken as matters of course; and is frequently silent as to those which are of the greatest importance, and which no seaman would pass over."

For instance, Luke mentions that when the ship was beached at Malta, the crew " unlashed the tiller ", and leaves it at that. A seaman would be much more likely to have explained how the tiller was secured. Again, if a sailor had written about the crew beginning to suspect that they were nearing land, he would surely have mentioned what indications there were. We are told that the ship's boat was secured " with difficulty ",[3] but we have no idea wherein the difficulty consisted—the chief detail which would interest any sailor.

On the other hand, it has been pointed out that St. Luke takes the greatest care to use the correct Greek word whenever he refers to the movements of a ship. No less than fourteen verbs, descriptive of the motion of a vessel at sea in particular circumstances,

[1] *St. Paul, the Traveller and Roman Citizen*, p. 206.
[2] *Op. cit.*, p. 22.   [3] Acts 27.16.

are found in his writings, and are not used by any
other New Testament authors.[1] This same love of
verbal accuracy on the part of St. Luke can be found
if his description of the storm on the Sea of Galilee is
compared with that of Matthew and Mark.

2. SHIPS

No details are given of the ships in which Paul and
his companions made their first three missionary
voyages. It may be taken for granted that they
were ordinary cargo vessels, carrying passengers. The
corn-ships, such as the one the centurion found at
Myra, were government vessels, used only by special
individuals, who, as we should say, had " priority "
over the ordinary travellers, e.g. members of the
Forces or Civil Servants.

The Roman and Graeco-Roman merchantmen at
the beginning of the Christian era depended almost
entirely on sail-power. It was only in the great war-
galleys that oars were used. In appearance these
Roman cargo ships did not differ very much from the
sailing craft of the Middle Ages. Their size varied
from small half-decked vessels used for short voyages
along the coasts, to larger ships able to carry from
120 to 200 tons of stores apiece. Only the Alexandrian
corn-ships were large enough to carry 276 persons on
board (the number in the vessel in which Paul was
wrecked at Malta), and about 250 tons of wheat.

It would appear that most ships were built of fir or
oak. The hull was constructed of planks fastened to
ribs, often with layers of skins to prevent leaks. The
joints were made with thin slips of wood, fitted into
mortices, inserted in the point faces of the planks, and
[1] Cf. James Smith, *op. cit.*, p. 28.

made fast with pegs. The bow and stern of the average sized cargo ship were more or less the same, slightly rounded; the stern-post less pronounced. Both bow and stern curved in gradually to meet the stem and stern-posts. Two or more heavy external timbers (wales) gave extra longitudinal strength to the hull above the water-line. The stern post curved upwards and was usually finished off with the head of a bird, generally a swan, looking aft.

The slightly curved stem projected above the bulwarks. In larger ships it was prolonged like a fighting-castle or look-out post. An eye was painted on each side of the bow, as is still the custom on most Mediterranean sailing-craft of the older type. The name or sign was also painted on the hull.

The build of such ships, also the rig, involved a great tendency to leak and the starting of planks. This defect is mentioned in many classical authors. For this reason, cables or chains had to be passed round the hull in bad weather, as related by St. Luke.[1]

Roman and Graeco-Roman ships were steered by two paddle-rudders, one on each quarter, acting in a rowlock or through a port-hole. Hinged rudders were not introduced until the Middle Ages. These oars or paddles were drawn up and housed when not in use. Steering was done by rotating the oar about its middle axis. The helmsman grasped a short handle set at right angles to the paddle.

Anchors varied in form. Some were without flukes. As we read in the Acts of the Apostles[2] the anchors were let down from the stern. Wall paintings at Herculanum and elsewhere show ships with stern

[1] Acts 27.17.
[2] 27.29.

anchors.   Small craft in the Greek islands still anchor at the stern.

In all but the larger ships there was only one mast, stepped amidships and more or less vertical.   It was securely stayed by four or more shrouds, and a heavy stay leaning forward.   The main yard was very heavy, and made of two spars, joined together at the centre.   Egyptian linen appears to have been used to form sail, which consisted of cloths placed horizontally and fitted with nine sets of brails or buntlines.   Sheets were run through rings, sewn on to the fore-side of the sail, so that it could be furled wholly or in part. There were braces to the yard-arms.   Lifts led to the mast-head from each yard-arm.   The gear was, on the whole, more clumsy than that used in after centuries.

Larger ships were provided with a foresail or *artemon*.   A foremast, more like a bowsprit, projected well over the bows.   This subsidiary sail helped ships to put about and have more speed.   Many of the larger vessels could keep up an average of seven nautical miles an hour, running before a wind.   A few large oars, or sweeps, were carried to turn the ship in harbour or to bring her head to wind in a light breeze.   This square rig was peculiarly favourable to making a quick run before the wind, but not so good when working to windward.   St. Luke mentions that " with the wind beating us back, we had to sail under the lee of Crete ".[1]   Many classical authors refer to the same difficulty.   A Graeco-Roman ship could not sail within seven points to the wind.   So far as we know the direction of the wind (which is fairly easy, provided that the time of year is certain) it is

[1] Acts 27.7.

possible to lay down the tacks of the ships in which Paul sailed on his voyages from Philippi to Troas[1]; from Sidon to Myra[2]; Myra to Gnidus[3]; from Salmone to Fair Havens[4]; and from Syracuse to Rhegium.[5]

The smaller ships, such as Paul would have made use of on his first missionary voyages, kept close to shore and never ventured on long sea courses. They seldom stayed long in any port, merely calling at one harbour or another to discharge or take on cargo. They depended on fitful land breezes and not on the prevailing winds that blew throughout the summer on the open sea.

3. THE FIRST MISSIONARY JOURNEY

Paul, accompanied by Barnabas and John Mark, set out from Antioch, at that date the third largest city in the Roman Empire, and made his way to the coast. About ten miles from Antioch was the port of Seleucia. The ruins of the town are situated on the top of a high hill. Two thousand years ago Seleucia was one of the greatest commercial ports on the Mediterranean—another Genoa, Marseilles or Alexandria. The port, which consisted of a great dock or basin, was connected with the sea by a canal. To-day the site is hidden by olive groves, for the sea receded many centuries ago.[6] Broken fragments of the limestone walls of the quays, also parts of the moles and the base of a lighthouse rise out of the ground. From one of those flights of stone steps among the trees, Paul and his fellow travellers must have boarded the ship in which they had booked their passage for Cyprus.

[1] Acts 20.6.   [2] 27.3–5.   [3] 27.6–7.   [4] 27.7–8.   [5] 28.12–13.
[6] Cf. note, p. 119.

The voyage must have been made in the early spring, as soon as the Mediterranean navigation had started that year; otherwise there would not have been an easterly wind to speed the little vessel on her course. She sailed out of the Bay of Antioch into the open sea. Astern of her rose up the lofty mountains of Asia Minor, merging into the Lebanon ranges to the south. No doubt she skirted the bold promontories and rugged cliffs of the Syrian coast. After several hours, given a stiff breeze, Paul and his shipmates, gazing westwards, would have made out the sharp mountain peaks of Cyprus rising above the horizon. The island is about seventy miles distant from the coast of Syria. The vessel could have made Cape Andreas in about nine or ten hours, maybe less.

Passing the Cape to the starboard, the helmsman set his course for Famagusta Bay, about thirty miles from the eastern tip of Cyprus. With an after wind the little ship would have been pitching the whole time.

Dense woods clothed the slopes of the mountains of Cyprus in ancient times. Against this green background, the white houses, palaces, temples and markets of Salamis stood out in vivid contrast. This maritime city was the commercial capital of Roman Cyprus and another busy port. To-day it is difficult, if not impossible, to picture its ancient splendour. The ruins of the great harbour, into which Paul's ship sailed, lie buried beneath sand dunes. Earthquakes, centuries ago, destroyed most of the ruins of the city.[1]

Having spent some time as the guests of the Jewish

[1] The modern port of Famagusta lies about five miles south of the ruins of Salamis.

community, engaged in the export of wine, copper, fruit and oil—no Mediterranean port lacked its Hebrew merchants at that period—the missionaries crossed the island and arrived at Paphos.[1]

In the first century of the Christian era, Paphos was the centre of government in Cyprus, a stately city set in a green valley by the sea. In the harbour, once filled with fleets of Roman warships and trading vessels, a few coasting-craft and fishing-boats are all that are left to remind one of the days of the past. North-east of the little town rises up the towering peak of Mount Troodos, the ancient Olympus. Ten miles to the east overlooking the Mediterranean, once stood a great temple, dedicated to Aphrodite, the goddess who came out of the sea-foam.

A ship had brought the first Christian missionaries to Cyprus. Many more ships brought pilgrims to these shores to venerate the black stone image of the sea-goddess.

In the harbour of Paphos, Paul found a ship bound for Asia Minor. It was now summer, and the prevailing winds had changed from east to west or south-west. So the vessel, having got out of the bay and steered through the islands, would have had an after wind as she skirted the coast towards Cape Arnauti (Orepanum), some twenty miles north of Paphos, and the western point of the island. As she moved on across the open sea, Mount Olympus sank lower and lower below the horizon. Then, sooner or later, Paul and his companions, had they been on the look-out, would have detected the high mountains of Pamphylia far away ahead of them. The distance from Paphos to Perge, whither they were bound, is

[1] The modern town of Kuklia.

about 170 miles. This now forgotten port was
situated at the head of the Gulf of Adalia.[1]   When the
travellers had landed, they journeyed through Asia
Minor and made their way back to Perge. Here
they boarded another ship in which they sailed for
Seleucia. This is a run of about 300 miles, which,
given a westerly wind, could have been covered in
less than two days. The vessel would have kept to
the north of Cyprus.

NOTE

It is a startling fact that hardly one of the many great
ports of the eastern Mediterranean frequented by shipping
during the first century of the Christian era exists to-day.
Vicente Ibanez (*Mare Nostrum*, English trans., p. 343)
points out how the sand, in so many places, has buried
even the foundations of once famous ports. Cities
renowned in history are to-day no more than streets of
ruins at the foot of a hillock crowned with the remains of
a Phoenician, Roman, Byzantine or Saracen castle, or
with a fortress contemporary with the Crusades. In
bygone centuries these had been famous ports; before
their walls had taken place naval battles; now from their
ruined acropolis one can scarcely see the Mediterranean
except as a light blue belt at the end of a low and marshy
plain. The accumulating sand has driven the sea back
for miles. Elsewhere inland cities have become places of
embarkation because of the continual perforation of the
waves. The wickedness of man has gone hand in hand
with the destructive work of nature. Nations have risen
and fallen in the course of two thousand years. Vast
harbours have been built, only to be destroyed by man or
by nature, or by both.

4.   THE SECOND MISSIONARY JOURNEY

The first part of the second missionary journey was
undertaken on land. When Paul eventually reached
Troas, on the north-west coast of Asia Minor, he was

[1] The modern port is Adalia.

joined by Luke. From now onwards this Greek physician was with him to note down the maritime incidents of travel.

The port of Troas consisted of a large basin, more than 400 feet long and 200 feet wide. It is now filled up and cut off from the sea. One night, Paul heard a voice entreating him to go over into Macedonia to preach the Gospel in Europe. So in answer to this mysterious call, he arranged with the master of a ship for a passage for himself and his party across the Aegean to Neapolis, a port about 100 miles from Troas.

We can picture this coasting-vessel being towed out of the basin, or her crew using the large oars which every sailing ship carried in those times. The square-sail was hoisted. She met the strong current between the mainland and Tenedos Island, which lay on the starboard bow. St. Luke tells us that she " made a straight course ", which indicates that there must have been a southerly wind. Far away to the west Paul and his fellow voyagers may have seen the peaks of Lemnos, supposing that the atmosphere was clear. Rounding Cape Marmara, the western point of Tenedos, the following wind helped the ship to make Imbros. With the wind from the south there was no danger of running into the broken waters of the Kharos Reef. The hills on Imbros, and the peak of Mount Elias, could be seen to the north. Keeping his eye on Avlaka Point, behind which rose up the 5,000-feet-high peak of Mount Fengari, on the island of Samothrace (Samothraski), the helmsman steered the ship on that " straight course ". Leaving Imbros astern, the steady breeze bore the vessel across the open Aegean. From the words used by St. Luke, " and the next day we made a course to Neapolis ", it suggests that the ship anchored off Samothrace for the night. The wind may have dropped after the sun went down.

The distance from Samothrace to Neapolis (the modern port of Kavala) is about seventy miles. If the vessel got under way at daybreak she could have made Neapolis by the same afternoon, given a following wind. She would pass the hilly, wooded island of Thasos on her starboard quarter. Far away to the west rise the jagged peaks of the peninsula of Mount Athos. Entering the Bay of Kavala, right ahead is the port of Neapolis. The distant view cannot have been very different from what it is to-day. But instead of the lofty promontory, on which the white houses rise in tiers, being crowned by a castle, Paul beheld a stately temple, dedicated to Venus. Behind the city is the encircling wall of the mountains of Macedonia.

Two thousand years ago, Neapolis was a busier port than the modern Kavala, where only a few cargo vessels and fishing-boats remind us of the fleets of Roman warships and merchantmen that once crowded the harbour.

Paul and his companions crossed the mountains to Philippi, about eight miles from the sea. Then they made their way by road to Thessalonica (the modern Salonika), another great commercial port. Having reached Beroea, now called Veria, an inland town on the west coast of the Gulf of Salonika, the Apostle had to flee from his enemies. " Whereupon the brethren sent Paul away, to continue his journey up to the coast ", writes St. Luke, who adds that " those who were escorting Paul on his journey saw him as far as Athens." Whether he made this journey by sea or by land is not clear. Some exegists make out that he may have reached the west coast of Greece, and from there found his way to Athens.

Five miles east of Corinth lies the Bay of Kekhries (Cenchreae), shut in by mountains. Through a gap in the hills, the bold mass of the Acro-Corinth—not unlike the Bass Rock or North Berwick Law in shape —is visible. An earthquake, many centuries ago, caused the harbour to disappear beneath the waves. When Paul came to Cenchreae from Corinth, accompanied by Aquila and Priscilla, to find a ship to take them to Ephesus, the Bay would have presented a very different appearance from what it does to-day. Two temples stood on the promontories; the one dedicated to Aphrodite, the other given over to the worship of Isis and Aesculapius. Right in the midst of the harbour was a great statue of Poseidon, the sea-god, holding a trident in one hand and a dolphin in the other.

The distance from here to Ephesus is nearly 300 miles, and the ship passed through the countless islands of the southern Aegean, hardly ever out of sight of land. It is easy to picture Paul, with his two friends, Aquila and Priscilla, beside him, sitting on the deck, watching the islands—Aegina, Zea, Thermia, Serpho and many another. Maybe they looked at the billowing sail of the vessel with critical eyes, for at Corinth they doubtless stitched sails as well as made tents.

After a week or more, their ship came within sight of the mainland. The mountains of Asia Minor lay ahead. She sailed into the Bay of Scalanova (Sinus Kaystrius) and anchored off Ephesus, a vast city

spread over the slopes of Mount Coresses, beneath
Mount Prion. In the distance Paul and his friends
saw the Temple of Diana, gorgeously decorated with
vivid colours and with the gold that shone in the
sunlight. The harbour at that date was a large basin,
connected with the sea by a canal, similar to the
harbours of Troas and Seleucia. It has long since
silted up and where the fleets were berthed at its
quays, are now dry land and marshes. This voyage
must have been taken in the late autumn, or more
likely in the very early spring, as soon as navigation
had started. We are told that Paul wanted to get
back to Jerusalem for the Passover, which in the year
53 A.D. fell on March 22nd. To reach his destination
in time he must have taken a ship carrying Jewish
pilgrims from Corinth. No doubt other pilgrims
boarded her at Ephesus, and she must have sailed
again almost immediately. The distance from Ephesus
to Caesarea, for which port she was bound, is about
600 miles. Given a fair wind, she could have crossed
the Mediterranean in time for these expatriated Jews
to assist at the Passover.

From the descriptions of life aboard medieval
pilgrim ships sailing to Palestine which have been
recorded, it is not difficult to visualize the squalor and
discomfort which must have been endured at sea by
pilgrims of an earlier age. There was very little
space and the ship was usually terribly overcrowded.
They slept, side by side, on mattresses. During the
day the bedding was rolled up, to afford space to move
about. One fifteenth-century pilgrim tells us that the
only light and ventilation came from the hatches,
which had to be battened down in rough weather, so

the place became " exceedingly hot and full of foul vapours ".[1] The bilge water had its own overpowering smell. Sleep, what with the moans of those who were seasick, others who were restless and persisted in moving from their beds, or the running about of the sailors overhead, was no easy matter. On deck, when it was fine, there was the heat of the sun; in the only public cabin, darkness, crowding, and tainted air. Vermin of all kinds crawled everywhere. Bread could not be kept fresh and hard biscuits formed the basis of every meal. Water was a luxury, for it could not be kept sweet for long in casks. Wine was more plentiful, and some pilgrims spent the greater part of the day getting drunk, if they were not gambling at cards or dice. This same pilgrim records: " I have marked it for a fact that the movement of all human passions is more violent on the water than else-where." Just as in the Middle Ages, so too in the times of the first Christian missionaries, women did not eat at the common table, but remained in their own quarters where they slept and ate. We read that, unless a man knows how to redeem the time on board a ship, he will find the hours very long and very tedious. Some passengers discuss their business, read, pray or meditate. Others run about, climb the rigging or play games. Some just sit and look at the sea and the land they are passing, and, like St. Luke, write about them afterwards. But the common occupation of all, passengers, officers and crew, was the loathsome, but most necessary, hunting and catching of lice and vermin. Such were the sort of conditions that Paul and the other Apostles would

[1] *The Wanderings of Felix Fabri*, Vol. I (Palestine Pilgrims' Text Society, Vol. VII).

have had to put up with on their missionary
voyages.

5. THE THIRD MISSIONARY JOURNEY

On his third journey, Paul, who was accompanied
by Timothy and other friends, travelled overland
across Asia Minor to the port of Ephesus.   Here they
boarded a ship bound for Neapolis.   Leaving the
harbour they sailed along the north coast of the island
of Samos for about twenty-five miles.   The rocky
peaks of its lofty mountains gleamed white against the
blue of the sky, their lower slopes being clothed with
forests.   About sixty miles north-east from Ephesus
they passed the bold headland of Cape Mastiko on
their starboard quarter;   it is the southern point of
Chios.   St. Luke, the Greek, must have gazed in
admiration at the rose-coloured hills of this large
island, dominated by Mount Elias.   Nine miles to the
north is Cape Amista, ending a line of bold cliffs.
Now the land fades away to starboard.   The following
wind keeps the vessel on a straight course, past Psara
Island;   then seventy miles of open sea, with no more
islands, except Strati rising up alone in the midst of
the Aegean, with the comparatively low mountains of
Lemnos twenty miles or so to the north-east.   Nearer
and nearer on the port bow looms up the mighty
cone of Mount Athos, over 5,000 feet high, its white
rocky peak looking like snow against the blue sky.
Another seventy miles of sailing, and the ship drops
anchor in the harbour of Neapolis (Kavala).   This
passage from Ephesus to Neapolis is about two hundred
miles.   Given a fair wind and no calms, it probably
took between two and three days.

Having landed in Macedonia, the missionaries

journeyed far and wide. Then they returned to the same port after they had kept the Passover at Philippi. It is probable that they set sail on April 15th. Four days later the ship made Troas, which shows that the winds must have been changeable, for the distance is no more than one hundred and twenty miles. Paul and his companions spent a week at Troas. He himself went on afoot to Assos; a twenty mile journey by road. His fellow missionaries took ship and sailed around the peninsula to meet him at Assos.

This port lies on the north shore of the Gulf of Adramyti, about nine miles east of the steep headland of Cape Baba (Lectum Promontorium). Facing Assos, across eight miles of water, are the mountains of Lesbos (Mytilene). Perhaps St. Paul, like H. V. Morton, found the Gulf of Adramyti, not its usual sapphire-blue, but with " waves the colour of lead, breaking on the rocks, and the wind screaming over the heights of Mytilene ".[1] For it was in the month of April when he stayed in this port. To-day only a few scattered ruins mark the site of Assos.

From now we can form a clearer picture of the rest of this voyage. Sailing from Assos on April 25th, the coasting-vessel in which the travellers had secured a passage dropped anchor the first night somewhere off the southern end of Mytilene. Next morning the helmsman kept her on a course south-south-west. Leaving Cape Zeitin (which he would have called Malea) astern, he steered for the headland at the north-west point of the Gulf of Smyrna; then onwards, until they " reached a point opposite Chios ".[2] Most likely they anchored in the strait between the island and the mainland, where they spent the night.

[1] *In the Steps of St. Paul*, p. 319. [2] Acts 20.15.

The following evening they " put in at Samos ", about forty miles south-east of the strait of Chios. On the third day after leaving Assos, the ship entered one of the four basins that made up the port of Miletus, at the mouth of the river Meander. The port has long since silted up and the ruins of the ancient capital of Ionia stand among desolate marshes. Several days were spent at Miletus.

" We tore ourselves away from the brethren ", says St. Luke, " and at last put out to sea." It was a " straight run " of about sixty miles from Miletus to the channel between Cos and the mainland. Then, bearing south for Cape Krio, the bold headland at the western end of the long Dorian peninsula, the ship sailed eastwards, with the island of Rhodes ahead. It is about fifty miles from Cape Krio, the ancient *Triopium Promontorium*, to the port of Rhodes. To starboard are the islands of Misiro and Tilos, with Symi to port.

It is hard to describe the islands of the Aegean as seen from the sea. They are of all shapes and sizes: so numerous that it is difficult to memorize them individually. H. V. Morton is right when he compares them to the Hebrides, strange as this may appear. But it is only at a distance that one often has the illusion of being off the west coast of Scotland instead of on the Mediterranean. A nearer view of any of the Aegean islands reveals something utterly different: rich vegetation on the lower slopes of many of them; little towns and villages with white-washed houses and red roofs; a profusion of flowers; vineyards and olive groves, and palm trees. It is in the late autumn or early spring, when the mists are rolling over

J

the mountains, or the sun shining after rain, that the islands of the Aegean really look like those of the West Highlands.

According to local tradition, Paul's ship did not put in to the main port of Rhodes, but turned south, making for the snug little harbour at Lindo. Here she would have been completely sheltered from westerly winds. Sailing due east for about sixty miles from Lindo she made Patara. This now forgotten port on the coast of Lycia, a few miles beyond the headland, known as the Seven Capes, was where Paul and his companions landed, the day after leaving Rhodes. The Bezan text of the Acts adds that the ship next put in to Myra about twenty miles farther east.

This coasting voyage from Troas to Myra was typical of the course taken by countless ships every summer. As H. Warrington Smyth reminds us, " navigation under sail in small craft has its drawbacks in a sea where the wind, even in weather of an apparently settled character, is liable to such sudden shifts as is the case of the Aegean. The sheltered anchorage of one hour is dead lee-shore the next; the greater the apparent protection when the anchor is dropped close in, the more imminent the danger when the wind is blowing a sudden gale right on the rocks. A southerly wind and fine weather may suddenly shift to due north with a heavy swell and confused sea, while six miles to the eastward a distant sail is seen with a fresh easterly wind."[1] Such were the weather conditions that the master of the coaster in which Paul took passage had to look out for.

[1] *Mast and Sail in Europe and Asia*, p. 319.

Myra, where Paul transhipped to another vessel, was one of the chief ports on the south coast of Asia Minor at that time. He would put in here on his voyage to Rome and once again change ships.

It was a great centre for the direct cross-sea traffic to and from Egypt and Syria. The harbour was seldom empty. Here Paul would have found Alexandrian corn-ships, Roman galleys, coasting-vessels, and fishing-boats. The streets around the harbour would be swarming with a cosmopolitan crowd of sailors. Myra was the seat of the sailors' god, to whom they offered their prayers before starting on the direct voyage and paid their vows on safe arrival; this devotion on the part of seafarers later found a Christian outlet in the cult of St. Nicholas of Myra, the patron saint of sailors, who held the same position in the maritime world of the Levant as St. Phokas of Sinope did in that of the Black Sea (where he was the Christianized counterpart of Achilles Pontarches, the Ruler of the Pontos).[1]

We cannot be certain, however, whether it was from Patara or Myra that Paul and his companions found a ship about to sail for Syria. St. Luke records[2] that " we sighted Cyprus, but passed it on the left, and held on for Syria, where we landed at Tyre, the port for which the vessel had shipped her cargo ". The distance from Patara to Tyre is about 350 miles. The vessel must have been one of the larger type of merchantmen that usually made direct passages instead of hugging the coast. The discharging of cargo kept the party at Tyre for a week. Here is the story of the departure from Tyre, as given by St. Luke:

[1] Ramsay, *St. Paul the Traveller*, p. 298.   See note, p. 130.
[2] Acts 21.3.

"All (the brethren), with their wives and children, escorted us until we were out of the city; and so we knelt down on the beach to pray; then, when farewells had been made on either side, we went on board ship, while they returned home."[1]

We can picture the little Christian community watching the ship sailing out of the harbour—perhaps they dared not gather in a body, lest they should be molested.

Given a fair wind, the voyage along the coast southwards to Caesarea would not have taken much more than three or four hours. After the missionaries had disembarked in the great harbour erected by Herod the Great, protected by its enormous break-water, they "went to the house of Philip the evangelist", and lodged there for several days, waited on by his four daughters. So ended the third journey of St. Paul the Apostle. His hosts implored him not to go up to Jerusalem, but he insisted on doing so.

NOTE

The voyages of the Apostles across the Mediterranean were the first stage in the eventual overthrow of the gods and goddesses of the sea, whose temples stood on the islands and headlands. The Christian sea apostolate, begun by St. Peter and the other fishermen of Galilee, and continued by the Apostle of the Gentiles, would, in the long run, lead to the destruction of those pagan shrines resorted to by Mediterranean mariners. Oceanus, the old god with the long beard, who lived in a cave, and had a vast family of sea-nymphs, the Oceanides, would be forgotten. So too their brother, Nereus, with his fifty daughters, the Nereids, who carried his orders over the waves and appeared to the crews of ships. There was Poseidon, master of the ocean, who took Amphitrite, the fairest of the Nereids, to be his wife. Poseidon was

[1] Acts 21.5–6.

believed to ride in his chariot over the sea, the hoofs of
his horses being the cause of the great waves that submerged
ships.   Many of the crews with whom the Apostles sailed
across the Mediterranean or coasted among the islands of
the Aegean, would have told them how they had seen
with their own eyes, or had met others who had seen,
Amphitrite, seated in her chariot of mother-of-pearl drawn
by the Tritons who were her sons.   Accompanying them
were their sisters the Naiads, who resembled mermaids.
Every seaport, every island and every headland had its
own particular god or goddess, which either watched over
ships and seamen or engulfed them in the waves.   Did
these sailors ever guess that among their passengers were
the leaders of a new religion that would dethrone the
maritime deities?

6. ST. PAUL'S VOYAGE TO ROME AND SHIPWRECK

Acts 27.1–6:

*And now the word was given for the voyage to Italy, Paul
being handed over, with some other prisoners, to a centurion
called Julius, who belonged to the Augustan cohort. We
embarked on a boat from Adrumetum which was bound for
the Asiatic ports, and set sail; the Macedonian, Aristarchus,
from Thessalonica, was with us.*

*Next day we put in at Sidon; and here Julius showed
Paul courtesy by allowing him to visit his friends and be
cared for.   Then, setting sail, we coasted under the lee of
Cyprus, to avoid contrary winds, but made a straight course
over the open sea that lies off Cilicia and Pamphylia, and
so reached Lystra, in Lycia.   There the centurion found a
boat from Alexandria which was sailing for Italy, and put
us on board.*

It has been reckoned from later dates given by
St. Luke that St. Paul and his companions sailed for
Italy on August 17th.   They embarked at Caesarea,

the chief seaport of Syria, and the nearest to Jerusalem. There were no local vessels large enough to take the party, so Julius, the centurion, made arrangements for them to embark on a cargo ship from Adrumetum, possibly Assos, which is on the Bay of Edremid (Adramyti), a seaport on the eastern shore of the Aegean, opposite Lesbos. A Christian community had been formed here by St. Peter, when he baptized the centurion Cornelius and his family.[1] St. Paul had been kept two years at Caesarea under Roman escort, to save him from the fury of the Jews, before he was sent to Rome.

The ship in which he embarked with other prisoners must have been homeward bound at this season of the year. Her normal course would be along the south coast of Asia Minor, where there were many flourishing ports. In one of them, the centurion Julius expected to find another ship to take his party to Italy.

After leaving Caesarea the ship made Sidon the following day. This was a distance of sixty-seven sea miles. The almost invariable S.W. wind that blows in late summer would have taken the vessel on the same course right to Sidon, which lies about N.N.E. of Caesarea. She probably called here for cargo. Julius allowed Paul to go ashore to meet this friends and to be cared for. May we suppose that they fitted him out with warm clothing for the autumn voyage?

Setting sail, the vessel was obliged to run under the lee of Cyprus, for the S.W. wind would be on their port side driving them to the coast of Cilicia. Then, favoured by light land breezes, they eventually reached Lystra, presumed to be the busy port of Myra. Here

[1] Acts 10.19–24.

they disembarked and took passage in one of the Alexandrian grain-ships, which was on her way to Italy. Westerly winds would force these great vessels to stand north from Egypt until they made Asia Minor. From here they expected a N.E. wind to take them to the Straits of Messina. Sometimes contrary winds delayed the voyages of the grain-ships for many weeks.

7. THE ALEXANDRIAN CORN-SHIPS

Contemporary representations of the Alexandrian corn-ships on medals, coins, and mural paintings at Pompeii and Herculanum, enable us to form a fairly clear idea of the type of vessel in which St. Paul made the last part of his voyage to Italy.

In general, they did not differ much from the ordinary Roman merchantmen described already (see p. 113), except that they were much larger. At each end of the ship was a trough-like projection, open at each end, forming a truncated quarter-gallery. They projected well over each quarter. Little information about the internal arrangements has been recorded. It is doubtful if there was a lower deck. The officers were accommodated in a large deck-cabin aft.

It was not often that one of the corn-ships took less than thirty-six days from Egypt to Italy. If they were forced to winter in Crete, Phoenice on the south-west coast was a safe harbour.

We know that there were 276 persons on board this ship, made up of soldiers, sailors and passengers. This may seem a large number, but it must be remembered that the average length of keel of a corn-ship was about 100 feet. It has been calculated that the average tonnage would be in the region of

1,000 tons.   About 250 tons of grain were carried in the holds.[1]

8.   ST. PAUL'S SAILING DIRECTIONS ARE IGNORED

Acts 27.7–12:

We had a slow voyage for many days after this; we made Gnidus with difficulty, and then, with the wind beating us back, had to sail under the lee of Crete by way of Salmone. Here we were hard put to it to coast along as far as a place called Fair Havens, near the city of Thalassa.

Much time had now been wasted, and sailing had become dangerous; the fast was already over, and Paul made them make the best of it.

" Sirs ", he said, " I can see plainly that there is no sailing now, without injury and great loss, not only of our freight and of the vessel, but of our own lives too."

The centurion, however, paid more attention to the helmsman and the master than to Paul's advice. The harbour was not well placed for wintering in; so that more of them gave their voices for sailing further still, in the hope of making Phoenice and wintering there; it is a harbour in Crete, which faces in the direction of the South-West and North-West winds.

After leaving Myra the grain-ship made little progress. The westerly wind beat her back again and again, and it was many days before she was off Knidos at the entrance of the Aegean Sea, a distance

[1] Cf. James Smith, *The Voyage and Shipwreck of St. Paul*; G. S. Laird Clowes, M.A., A.I.N.A., *Sailing Ships: their history and development as illustrated in the collection of the Science Museum*; A. Breusing, *Die Nautik der Alten*; J. Vars, *L'Art nautique dans l'Antiquité*; F. Vigouroux, *Le Nouveau Testament et les découvertes archéologiques modernes*; A. Trève, *Une traversée de Cesarée de Palestine à Puteolis au temps de S. Paul*.

of about 130 geographical miles.[1]   With a fair wind
the Aegean could have been made in one day.

Then the wind shifted to N.N.W.   There was
nothing to do but beat back to the south side of
Crete, past the lofty islands of Karpathos, Scarpanto,
Kasos, and other islands of the Cyclades.   Modern
sailing directions warn mariners that N.W. winds may
be expected in the summer months, especially in the
eastern half of the Mediterranean.   Having passed
Cape Sidero at the north-eastern end of Crete, the
ship was in smoother waters, but the westerly current
which flows here would have reduced her speed, even
with a favourable breeze.

There were squalls too, and it was only after many
days that they anchored in a bay about three miles
eastward of Cape Littinos, to-day known as Kalo
Limiones (Fair Havens).   It lies open to the eastward,
but is partly sheltered by two small islands.   " It is
not recommended as an anchorage to winter in;
although a vessel well found in anchors and chains,
as in the present day, would have a better chance than
in the days of St. Paul, by securing with stern-fasts to
the shore, under the lee of, or on the northern side of
the islet of St. Paul."[2]   Here the ship seems to have
remained for over three weeks, for, as St. Luke
says, " much time had now been wasted ".   The
" dangerous season " for sea navigation began on
September 14th, after which the almost unvarying
equinoxial gales started.   After November 11th, all
navigation ceased until the spring.

The officers seem to have been unable to decide

---

[1] Knidos (Gnidus) was a Greek city at the western tip of the
Dorian peninsula, north-west of the island of Rhodes.

[2] *Mediterranean Pilot*, Vol. IV, p. 63.

whether to remain at Fair Havens or to sail on to Phoenice (Port Lutro), where there was a safe harbour. St. Paul warned them that if they sailed there was danger of losing the ship as well as the lives of passengers and crew. But the centurion felt he had no alternative than to act on the advice of the ship's master, who wanted to make a safer harbour.

It may be supposed that the master was annoyed at a mere landsman, even more a prisoner, expressing such positive opinions on nautical matters—what could he know about winter gales and the seaworthiness of Alexandrian grain-ships? It must have seemed almost an insult to his rank as the commander of one of these vessels. As others agreed with the master that the best thing to do was to sail westwards, the centurion, who had the final word, gave orders that the ship was to raise anchor and hoist sail.

9.   THE STORM AT SEA

Acts 27.13–20:

A light breeze was now blowing from the South, so that they thought they had achieved their purpose, and coasted along Crete, leaving their anchorage at Assos. But it was not long before a gale of wind struck the ship, the wind called Euraquilo. She was carried out of her course, and could make no head against the wind, so we gave up and let her drive. We now ran under the lee of an island named Cauda, where we contrived, with difficulty, to secure the ship's boat. When it had been hoisted aboard, they strengthened the ship by passing ropes round her; then, for fear of being driven on to the Syrtis sands, they let down the sea-anchor, and so drifted.

On the next day, so violently were we tossed about in the

gale, they lightened ship, and on the third day threw the spare tackle overboard.

For several days we saw nothing of the sun or the stars, and a heavy gale pressed us hard, so that we had lost, by now, all hope of surviving; and we were much in want of food.

The following morning a moderate southerly wind was blowing. So the command was given to weigh anchor, and the ship sailed close in under the land until she was past Cape Matala, about six miles from Fair Havens. We can picture the helmsman and those on deck on this bright autumn morning, keeping an eye on the wind, the lofty mountains and the cape ahead. If the wind went round a point towards west, they would never round Cape Matala. However, they did so and found themselves in open waters, for the coast turns directly north for about ten miles after the Cape has been passed. The course was set across the Bay of Messera, Phoenice being about thirty miles north-west, close under the bold range of the Madara or White Mountains.

The ship must have been about half way across the Bay, not far from the two little islands of the Paximades, when the wind shifted to the north-east. A sudden squall burst. The typhonic wind, known as Euraquilo, swept down from the 7,000-feet-high peak of Mount Ida and struck the vessel with terrific force.[1] A ship of this type, with one huge sail, was in the utmost danger from such a blast, the strain on the sail on the single mast being more than the hull could bear. These ancient wooden vessels ran the risk of foundering in the open sea. In a whirlwind like this, the crew

[1] Such gales are very frequent in the autumn and winter.

would have been unable to slacken sail quickly. The helmsman could not keep the ship to wind, for the strain would have shaken her to bits. The only thing to do was to let her drive.

So she surged and plunged onwards for some twenty miles, with the waves threatening to poop her. The small mountainous island of Cauda (Clauda), now called Gavdo, lay ahead. They managed to turn the ship's head to wind and reached calmer waters under the lee of the high cliffs on the southern coast of this island. Here the sails were trimmed. All this time the ship's boat had been towed and she was water-logged. We read that it was only with great difficulty that the crew managed to hoist her aboard and make her fast.

Then the sailors girded the ship to strengthen her timbers, passing four or five turns of cable-laid rope round her hull. Next they lowered the gear, presumably the top-sails normally hoisted only in fine weather. In Mgr. Knox's translation he adds the words that " they let down the sea-anchor, and so drifted ".

What the master and crew feared was that they would be driven on to the dangerous quicksands of the Desert of Syrtes on the coast of North Africa, between Tripoli and Benghazi. In this case, the vessel would be a total wreck. Were the gale to last much longer, this would be almost inevitable.

The wind, which had first been an eddying blast from the mountains of Crete, had now turned into a steady N.E. gale. It would appear that the ship was put on to the starboard tack, with stormsails set, drifting with her head to the north. Next day she was rolling so violently that orders were given to lighten ship, which implies that cargo was thrown overboard. The waves were hitting her broadside on, and vessels of this type could ill stand such a constant straining of their timbers. The weather showed no signs of changing the following morning. Both passengers and crew (so the Authorised Version implies by the use of the first person plural) threw the spare tackle overboard, i.e. the long, heavy mainyard, unless we are mistaken. (Acts 27.19.) The panic on board must have increased.

Eleven days and nights elapsed. The sky was overcast; low clouds hid the stars, and with no compass to guide the helmsman, those on board had no idea in what direction the ship was drifting. There was no means of getting bearings. The gale continued; the vessel was driven onward and onward like a drunken man. There were nearly three hundred persons on board this ship, and they had not been able to get much to eat or drink for nearly a fortnight. In such weather, with the seas breaking over the vessel, it would have been impossible to cook any food. Very likely the caboose, or galley, had been washed away. The crew were worn out with long hours at the pumps. Both they and the passengers began to lose hope of ever reaching land alive.

10. ST. PAUL PROMISES THERE WILL BE NO LIVES
LOST ON BOARD

Acts 27.21–26:

Now Paul stood up in their presence, and said: " Sirs, you should have taken my advice; if you had not put out from Crete, you would have saved all this injury and damage. But I would not have you lose courage, even now; there is to be no loss of life among you, only of the ship. An angel stood before me last night, sent by the God to whom I belong, the God whom I serve, and said, ' Have no fear, Paul, thou

art to stand in Caesar's presence; and behold God has granted
thee the safety of all thy fellow voyagers'. Have courage
then, sirs; I trust in God, believing that all will fall out as
he has told me.   Only we are to be cast up on an island."

11.   ST. PAUL BIDS THE CENTURION TO KEEP THE
CREW ON BOARD, AND CARES FOR THE PASSENGERS

Acts 27.27–38:

On the fourteenth night, as we drifted about in the Adriatic
sea, the crew began to suspect, about midnight, that we were
nearing land.   So they took soundings, and made it twenty
fathom: then they sounded again, a short distance away, and
made it fifteen fathom.   Afraid, therefore, that we might be
cast ashore on some rocky coast, they let down four anchors
from the stern, and fell to wishing it were day.

And now the sailors had a mind to abandon the ship, and
lowered the boat into the sea, pretending that they meant to
lay out anchors from the bows.   But Paul told the centurion
and the soldiers: " These must stay on board, or there is no
hope left for you."   Whereupon the soldiers cut the boat's
ropes away and let it drop.

As the day began to break, Paul entreated them all to take
some food: " To-day", he said, " is the fourteenth day you
have been in suspense, and all that time gone hungry, neglecting
to eat; pray take some food, then; it will make for your
preservation; not a hair of anyone's head is to be lost."

And with that he took bread, and gave thanks to God before
them all, and broke it, and began to eat.   Thereupon they all
found courage, and themselves took a meal.   The whole
number of souls on board was two hundred and seventy-six.
So all ate till they were content ; and afterwards they began
to lighten the ship, throwing the corn into the sea.

Only Paul kept his head.   He saw that his shipmates
were starving, and weak from lack of food.   He

reminded them that they had not had a proper meal for a fortnight and that all this time their nerves had been on edge. He gave orders that breakfast, such as it was, must be got ready. Nobody need worry any more. In an hour or two they would be safe on dry land. The 276 persons on board—soldiers, sailors, passengers and prisoners—began to eat, after Paul had procured enough bread. But before this he " gave thanks to God before them all, and broke the bread ", thus turning this meal into the partaking of a sacrament. When they had satisfied their hunger their courage returned. No longer were they afraid. For the moment they forgot those fourteen days and nights which they had endured, with a never ending terror that they would be drowned.

Now they set to work to lighten the ship still more, going down into the holds, throwing corn into the sea.

The great gale had raged for nearly a fortnight. About midnight while the ship was still drifting on the dark and raging waters of the Adriatic, as this part of the Mediterranean was called in those days,[1] the sailors were convinced that land was near. No doubt they heard the roar of the breakers on the rocks. Soundings were taken; there could no longer be any doubt that land was not far off.[2]

[1] See note, p. 148.

[2] James Smith in *The Voyage and Shipwreck of St. Paul* (4th ed. 1880, pp. 126–127) has proved very conclusively after consulting several nautical experts that the mean rate of the drift of a ship like that in which St. Paul was sailing, would have been from $3\frac{3}{4}$ miles an hour to 2 miles an hour in a N.E. gale. He points out that the ship had taken almost exactly thirteen days from Cauda to Malta, a distance of 476·6 miles. At the above reckoning of drifting (33 miles to 36 miles in 24 hours) the time works out to 13 days 1 hour. He is satisfied that if the ship started late in the evening from Cauda, it would be midnight on the fourteenth day when she was less than three miles from the entrance to St. Paul's Bay on the east coast of Malta.

The master of the ship began to fear that she would
be driven on to the rocks. When dawn broke he
gave orders that four anchors were to be let down
from the stern. Roman ships, so it would appear
from paintings and engravings on medals and rings,
were fitted with hawse-holes both forward and aft;
the latter also acting as rudder ports. The hawsers
were coiled round the upright beam of the stern post.
The number of anchors shows that nothing was left
to chance. Had the ship been anchored by the bow,
she might have swung round from wind. It would
have been difficult to manage her with the bow
pointing to wind and away from the shore, if the
master had decided to beach her. All that had to
be done with the anchors at the stern, was to cut the
cables, unlash the rudders, hoist the foresail or artemon,
and the ship could be beached anywhere.[1]

There was nothing more that could be done. The
crew waited for daylight: then they would be able to
see what land they had drifted to, and what chances
there were of saving the ship and getting ashore.
The sun rose, and those on deck discovered that they
were at the entrance of a bay of considerable depth,
maybe two miles. Had the wind been off-shore there
would have been a safe anchorage, but it was still
blowing from the N.E., and the waves were thundering
on the beaches and breaking over the rocky cliffs.

The sailors, deciding that there was little chance of
safety if they remained on board the ship, lowered the
boat, on the pretext of laying out other anchors from
the bow. Paul noticed them, and informed the
centurion and the soldiers. He assured them that
there was no hope for them unless they remained on

[1] Cf. Ramsay, *op. cit.*, p. 335.

" I am going out fishing . . ." [*John 21.3*]

"So they cast the net, and found before long they had no strength left to haul it in, such a shoal of fish was in it" [*John 21.6*]

the ship. So the soldiers cut the boat's ropes and cast her adrift. It seems that, by this time, Paul had practically taken command of the ship, and that the centurion was prepared to obey his orders.

He stood up before the officers and the crew, and had the courage to remind them that, if they had taken his advice and not sailed from Fair Havens, the ship would still have been riding safely at anchor in that harbour. He bade them not to abandon hope, and assured them that no lives would be lost, only the ship herself. He told them that he had received a message from an angel the night before, and that God would preserve all those who were in the ship. "Don't be afraid! I believe in God, and that all will happen as was revealed to me last night by this angel. I can tell you with certainty that we shall be washed up on to an island!"

12. THE SHIPWRECK

Acts 27.39-44:

When day broke, they found that the coast was strange to them. But they sighted a bay with a sloping beach, and made up their minds, if it should be possible, to run the ship ashore there. They lifted the anchors and trusted themselves to the mercy of the sea, at the same time unlashing the tiller; then they hoisted the foresail to the breeze, and held on for the shore. But now, finding they were running into a cross sea, they grounded the ship where they were. The bows, which were stuck fast, felt no movement, but the stern began falling to pieces under the violence of the waves.

The soldiers would have killed the prisoners, for fear that any of them should dive overboard and escape, but the centurion baulked them of their will, because he had a mind to keep Paul safe. He gave orders that those who could swim

K

should go overboard first, and make their way to land; of the
rest, some were ferried across on planks, and some on the
ship's wreckage.   So it was that all reached land in safety.

It was now broad daylight and the details of the
coast could be made out clearly, but nobody could
recognize the land.   On the north side of the bay
there was a sandy beach.   The master of the ship
decided to try to run her aground on this spot.   He
gave orders to cut the anchor hawsers.   The sailors
hoisted the fore-sail, and unlashed the rudder.   The
ship drifted towards the shore.   Before long she was
rolling heavily in a cross sea, opposite to the narrow
channel between a small island and the mainland.
A hundred yards or so ahead was the beach.   In a
few moments she was aground, with her bow stuck
fast in the stiff clay, formed of the disintegrated rocks
from the low cliffs.   The waves broke against the
stern, and it began to break up, for after battling
through the great gale, the ship was badly strained
and leaking.

The centurion would not allow the soldiers to kill
the prisoners (as they wished to, lest they should escape),
being anxious to make sure of the safety of Paul: such
a remarkable man might be useful to him in the near
future.   It was he who had, to all intents and purposes,
assumed command of the ship when all had lost heart
and believed themselves to be lost.   The centurion
bade all who could swim to jump overboard.   Others
managed to grab hold of broken wreckage or planks
of wood, and thus reached dry land.   The 276 persons
eventually found themselves safe and sound on the
island of Malta.   Such at least has been the almost
universally accepted opinion throughout the centuries.

13. SAFE ON LAND

Acts 28: v. 1:

When we were safe on land, we found that the island was called Melita. The kindness which the natives shewed to us was beyond the ordinary.

vv. 7–14:

Among the estates in that part were some which belonged to the leading citizen of the island, a man named Publius, who took us in and for three days entertained us hospitably; and it so happened that Publius' father had taken to his bed, laid up with fever and dysentery. Paul, who had gone to visit him, laid his hands upon him with prayer, and healed him; whereupon all the other folk in the island who were suffering from infirmities came to him and found a cure. They paid us great honour, and when we embarked they loaded us with all the supplies we needed.

It was at the end of three months that we sailed, in a ship from Alexandria which had wintered at the island; its sign was Castor and Pollux. We put in at Syracuse, where we waited for three days; then we coasted round the further shore, and so arrived at Rhegium. When we had spent a day there, a south wind came on, and we made Puteoli on the second day out. Here we found some brethren, who prevailed on us to stay with them for a week. And so ended our journey to Rome.

It was only after they had landed that they discovered that they were on the island of Melita, now known as Malta. Almost every topographical detail given by St. Luke corresponds to the features of St. Paul's Bay on the north side of the island, about five miles from Mdina (Notabile), the ancient fortified capital. Melita had been colonized by several nations during its long history, including the Phoenicians, Greeks and Carthaginians. The Romans had taken possession of the island in 218 B.C. It was Publius, the governor, who

entertained the shipwrecked mariners, soldiers and
prisoners after the natives had shown " kindness that
was beyond the ordinary ".   Paul cured the father of
Publius who was suffering from a fever and dysentery,
and also healed many other persons of their diseases.[1]

The shipwreck had taken place before the middle
of November.   The travellers were detained in Malta
about three months.   There happened to be another
Alexandrian corn-ship wintering in one or other of the
two great natural harbours.   St. Luke mentions the
name of this vessel—*Dioscuri* (The Two Brothers, i.e.
Castor and Pollux).   He must often have looked at
her, and her name became fixed in his memory.   He
does not tell us the names of the other ships.   " He
had not the sailor's mind, who thinks of his ship as a
living friend, and always speaks of her by name:
hence the other ships were to him only means of
conveyance, whereas the name of the *Dioscuri* was the
first fact he learned about her."[2]

About the middle of February, Paul and his companions were ordered aboard the *Dioscuri*, and she
sailed for Italy.   This was earlier than usual for sea
navigation, but there must have been a favourable
wind, probably from the south or south-west, otherwise
the voyage would not have been attempted.   Leaving
Malta astern, granted that the land was not hidden
by clouds, it would not have been very long before
they noticed Monte Lauro, the highest peak of the

[1] The generally accepted date of St. Paul's shipwreck is the year 58.
There is a legend that he consecrated Publius as first Bishop of
Malta.   The latter is supposed to have been martyred towards the
end of the first century.   The feast of " St. Paul Shipwrecked " is
celebrated at Malta on February 19th as a Double of the 2nd Class.
Other local feast-days associated with St. Paul's voyages are: his
(supposed) landing at Reggio Calabria (May 21st), and his coming
to Pozzuoli (May 30th).

[2] Ramsay, *op. cit.*, p. 346.

Iblei Mountains of Sicily, rising up above the northern horizon. Steering past Cape Passero (the ancient Promontorium Pachynum), at the S.E. point of Sicily, and rounding what is now called the Penisola della Maddalena, the helmsman would bring the vessel into the great harbour of Syracuse. Given a fair wind, the corn-ship could have made this hundred-mile passage in twenty-four hours.

Three days were spent at Syracuse. Then the anchors were raised, the sails hoisted and, presuming that there was still a southerly wind, the course set for the coast of Calabria. Thence, by tacking north they made Rhegium, now known as Reggio Calabria. Thanks to a sirocco—the warm south wind from North Africa—the ship was able to sail through the Straits of Messina, which would have been impossible had the wind been in another direction. There are rapid currents which sweep past the headland of Scilla, causing dangerous eddies and even whirlpools when there is a gale blowing.

From the Straits of Messina to the Bay of Naples is a distance of about 180 nautical miles. The corn-ship could have made this run in any time between twenty-four hours and two days, according to the force and the direction of the wind. St. Luke tells us that the south wind blew all the time, and that they made Puteoli the next day. They would have passed close to the island of Stromboli, with its smoking volcano. Then, perhaps six or nine hours later, they would have made out the long range of mountains on the Peninsula of Sorrento, away to the north-east. To the north-west the island of Capri rose out of the sea. Steering between Capri and Punta Campanella, the ship entered the Bay of Naples. About eighteen miles distant, at the far north of the Bay, lay Puteoli—the modern Pozzuoli—then the chief port in Italy south of Ostia at the mouth of the Tiber. Seneca[1] describes the arrival of the corn-ships from Egypt at Puteoli. He tells us that all ships entering the Bay were obliged to strike their topsails, except the corn-ships. Thus the latter vessels would be distinguished at a great distance. Fast sailing craft (*tabellariae*) were sent forward to announce the coming of any vessels of the fleet from Alexandria, so that men would be in readiness to discharge the cargoes.

As in so many other Mediterranean seaports, by A.D. 67 there was a Christian community at Puteoli. They soon heard of the landing of Paul and his companions, and made them welcome. The travellers spent a week in this port. Then they continued their journey to Rome by road, by way of Terracina. News of them must have gone on ahead, for " the brethren " came out to meet the party as far as " Appius' Market " and the " Three Taverns ". When Paul saw them he thanked God and regained his courage. Some hours later they entered Rome by the Appian Gate.

NOTE

It would appear that, even before the Christian era, the word Adria, i.e. the Adriatic Sea, had taken on a much wider meaning than the gulf north of the Straits of Otranto, lying between the east coast of Italy and Dalmatia. Sailors used the word Adria to comprise what is now called the Ionian Sea, i.e. the stretch of water north of a line drawn from the south coast of Sicily to Cape Matapan in Greece (cf. James Smith, *op. cit.*, Appendix VI). " It is quite unnecessary that we should expect from St. Luke, in his purely casual expression, anything else than conformity with common language."

[1] *Epistle* 77.

CHAPTER VIII

THE MARITIME SYMBOLISM OF
THE EARLY CHRISTIAN CHURCH

THE MARITIME SYMBOLISM OF
THE EARLY CHRISTIAN CHURCH

Bidding us poor wanderers to cling to the hope we have in view, the anchorage of our souls—Hebrews 6.18.

Look at the ships; how huge they are, how boisterous are the winds that drive them along! And yet a tiny rudder will turn them this way and that, as the captain's purpose will have it—James 3.4.

The kingdom of heaven is like a net that was cast into the sea, and enclosed fish of every kind at once—Matthew 13.47.

THE close association of the sea with the spread of the Gospel was not forgotten by the early Christians. It was in the chief commercial ports around the eastern Mediterranean that most of the first Christian communities were established. The same wind that blew the seeds of Egyptian plants to Italy, filled the sails of the ships that bore Peter, the fisherman, and Paul, the native of a great world-seaport, to Rome.

When the Christians began to be persecuted, and were forced to worship underground, they covered the walls of the Catacombs with maritime symbols. A ship or boat became the symbol of the Church herself. It had been used by the Egyptians, Greeks and Romans as a pagan symbol of human life; now it was given a new meaning. To those who glanced up at the paintings or the rude incisions on the walls of the Catacombs, the ship reminded them that, so long as they remained on board the Church, they were certain of reaching a safe port. Sometimes the ship is depicted sailing towards a lighthouse: the Christian soul, supported by Christ, borne across the waves and weathering the storms of life. Or these little vessels, with or without sails, could be regarded as the emblems of the Church, driven to and fro, but never foundering. The Cross was her standard. She was driven forward by the wind of the Holy Spirit and carried a precious freight of souls. As St. Hippolytus wrote in the third century after Christ: " The world is a sea, in which the Church, like a ship, is beaten by the waves, but not submerged." St. Clement of Alexandria, who had sailed all over the eastern Mediterranean, had a ship engraved on his ring. " Let the dove, or the fish, or the vessel flying before the wind—or the marine anchor—be our signets."[1] In the *Apostolic Constitutions*,[2] the bishop surrounded by the faithful is compared to the helmsman of a ship. The same idea is expressed by Tertullian.[3] Elsewhere the Church is compared to the Ark of Noe.

Abbot Cabrol[4] quotes part of a document " anterior to the fourth century " in which this ship-symbolism is stressed.

" When you assemble the church of God, think of yourself [the author is addressing a bishop in the name of the Apostles] as the captain of a great ship, and so order all things with prudence, commanding the deacons to arrange the brethren according to their rank.

" Firstly, the church shall resemble a ship; it shall

[1] *Paedagogus*, III, 2; *P.G.*, VIII, 633.
[2] II, 47.
[3] *De. baptismo*, XII; *P.L.*, I, 1214.
[4] *Liturgical Prayer*, p. 60.

be long, turned to the east, and having a room on each side.

" The seat for the bishop must be in the middle, the priests seated on either side, and the deacons standing lightly clad as befits those who must be always at work about the ship. . . . When the Gospel is being read, the priests, deacons, and all present shall stand in silence. This reading shall be followed by an exhortation to the people, each of the priests preaching in his turn, and after them the bishop, as captain of the ship."

The anchor was an even more popular Christian symbol in the first centuries. It is the most ancient symbol found in connection with Christian epigraphs, and expressed the idea of hope, confidence, and safety. The preachers, as well as many of their congregations, had personal experience of the value of anchors during those stormy passages on the Mediterranean, or when their little ships were seeking a safe refuge in some bay or harbour on one of the many islands of the Aegean. The Catacombs are filled with representations of anchors, most of which belong to the third century. They are either cruciform or in the shape of tridents. The former type is most common. Very often two fishes are shown on either side of the anchor. In some cases a single fish is twisted round the shaft of the anchor—a symbol of the Crucifixion. After the fourth century, the anchor gradually disappeared as a common Christian symbol; the cross replaced it.

A fish was an expression of belief in the divinity of Christ. It was bound up with an acrostic, consisting of the initial letters of five Greek words, forming the word *ichthus*, i.e. Jesus Christ, Son of God, Saviour. Those who believed in the Divine Fish—the *Ichthus*—

were regarded as " little fishes after the image of our Fish, Jesus Christ, and born in the water ". Or to put it differently: Christian souls, swimming towards that which is the centre and lodestone of their affection —the Cross of Christ, symbolized by the anchor. The fish also became a symbol of the Holy Eucharist, and was thus used on seals, rings, cruets, and on the walls of places of worship. It was a reminder, too, of the stories in the Gospels of the miraculous feeding of the five thousand and the four thousand men on the shores of the Sea of Galilee with a few loaves and small fishes, each incident prefigured the spiritual feeding on the Body and Blood of Christ.

Less common, but used occasionally, was a fishing-net —another symbol of the Church. What must never be forgotten is the fact that it was the symbols of sailors and fishermen—the material objects which were most closely associated with the toil and drudgery of working men who earned their living by the sea, which were even more common among the first Christians than emblems connected with the land.

Worshippers in the Catacombs did not forget the close association with Christ and the sailor. They remembered that the Prince of the Apostles had mended and shot nets before he had handled the keys of the kingdom of heaven; that he had caught fish before he cast his hook for men. As they looked around those dark subterranean places of worship they were confronted by maritime objects—ships, boats, anchors, lighthouses, fishes and nets. It never struck them that there was anything odd in this form of decoration. To-day pious members of any congregation might complain that such objects are devoid of any devotional stimulus; that they would be more suitable in a fishmonger's shop than in a church. It has been forgotten that, in a very real sense, the Church started as a Mission to Fishermen.

We do not know when St. Peter came to Italy, or at what port he landed first. No precise details of his sojourn in Rome have been recorded, but traditions, some of which date from the first half of the second century, suggest that he found his way to Italy after he had been liberated from prison in Jerusalem. As likely as not the fisherman-Apostle took passage in a ship which discharged her cargo at Ostia, at that time one of the largest and richest ports on the Mediterranean. Situated at the mouth of the Tiber, about sixteen miles from Rome, was a vast city, known as Portus Romanus. The Emperor Claudius had built the first harbour among the marshes. To Ostia, even more than to Puteoli, came the corn-ships from Egypt. Trade was carried on from here with all parts of the Mediterranean.

If you make your way from Rome to Ostia and sit on the sandy beach, you can picture a ship with its sail billowing out with south-westerly wind bringing the fisherman-Apostle from Palestine to Italy. Away to the south a long line of pine woods rise above the sandy dunes. To the east, beyond the wide expanse of desolate marshes, are the distant peaks of the Apennines. About a mile inland, for the sea has receded in the course of nineteen centuries, are the ruins of Portus Romanus—granaries, barracks, theatres, temples and offices of the shipping companies. It is practically certain that Peter walked through these streets and along the quays. His feet must have stood on those mosaic pavements decorated with ships, tridents, dolphins and sea-gods.   To-day the ruins are deserted.   It is only the sharp clicking of grasshoppers, the slithering movements of lizards, or the soughing voice of the wind that break the silence.   For Ostia was abandoned long, long ago.   It has something of that eerie atmosphere that is found to-day in the blitzed seaport of Saint-Nazaire, where hardly a house has been left standing, and where one is haunted by the ghosts of seafarers.

If St. Peter's ship put into Ostia and discharged her cargo, it is possible that he went aboard a smaller vessel and sailed up the Tiber to Rome.   Supposing that it was at Ostia that he landed on the soil of Italy for the last time before he took up his permanent residence in Rome, it was on this spot that he bade farewell to the sea.   On the other hand it is more than probable that a Christian community was formed at Ostia at an early date—the " brethren " were always more numerous in seaports than in inland towns. Such being the case, then St. Peter would have paid periodical visits to the mouth of the Tiber and mingled with the sailors.

According to a venerable tradition Peter the fisherman lived in Rome, on and off, for about twenty-five years.   Among his first converts was the senator Cornelius Pudens.   Most of this noble family were baptized by St. Peter.   It was Quintus Cornelius Pudens and his wife, Priscilla, who took the Apostle into their home and looked after him.   In the early Middle Ages the Church of S. Pudentiana was built on the site of this house.   The modern pilgrim who visits it is told that the marble columns in the nave were taken from the house of Pudens.   As one gazes up at the ninth-century mosaics which glow in the dark apse one can meditate on all that must have taken place on this spot nineteen centuries ago. " Here, St. Peter celebrated the sacred mysteries, presided at the synaxes or assemblies of the faithful, approved the Gospel written by his disciple, St. Mark, and consecrated St. Linus and St. Cletus, who were his successors. . . . We may try to recall the scene which that blessed home presented in those ancient days—St. Peter in a long vestment, celebrated the holy mysteries in the atrium of Pudens' palace. . . . The senator Pudens and his wife, Priscilla, kneel there, side by side, with their young son, Pudens, whom St. Peter had baptized. The lady Pomponia Graecina, wife of Aulus Plautius, is probably there also, for she, too, is a devout Christian. They kneel or stand, with arms extended, that being the attitude of prayer among the early Christians, as represented in the frescoes of the catacombs."[1]

Historians are not agreed about the truth of the tradition associating St. Peter with the palace of Pudens that stood on the site of the Church of S. Pudentiana. There is more certainty that he administered baptism and preached to the faithful in the Catacomb of St. Priscilla on the Via Salaria outside the city walls. The catacomb lies beneath the foundations of a first-century villa. In it were buried the bodies of many martyrs, including SS. Pudens, Priscilla and Pudentiana.

At first the Christian community in Rome was more or less unmolested. After Nero had been declared emperor in A.D. 54 persecution started, and by the time that St. Paul reached Rome in A.D. 61, he was

[1] P. J. Chandlery, S.J., *Pilgrim-Walks in Rome*, 2nd edition, 1905, pp. 106–107.

kept under guard, although he was allowed to meet his disciples.   Four years later, so St. Ambrose relates,[1] the Christians began to fear for the safety of St. Peter. They persuaded him to leave Rome and seek refuge in the country.   According to the legend the old fisherman crept out of the city one dark night, and took the Appian Way southward.   About two miles from the walls he beheld his Divine Master walking in towards him.   " Lord," he said, " whither goest thou? "   Jesus looked at his aged disciple and replied: " I go to Rome to be crucified anew."   Then he vanished.   St. Peter felt that this was a reproof for his impetuosity.   He turned around and retraced his steps to the city.   Not long afterwards he was arrested and cast into prison.

It would be almost impossible to find a more horrible place of confinement than the Mamertine Prison, where, according to tradition, SS. Peter and Paul remained for eight or nine months.   It consists of two underground dungeons, the one below the other, " with only one round aperture in the centre of each vault, through which alone light, air, food, and men could pass.   When the upper story was full, we may imagine how much light and air could reach the lower. No other means of ventilation, drainage, or access existed.   The walls, of large stone blocks, had rings fastened into them for securing the prisoners, but many used to be laid on the floor with their feet fastened in stocks ".[2]   If the two Apostles were imprisoned in the lower dungeon as is popularly supposed, " it would be hard to imagine a spot more appalling. . . .   The thick darkness, the fetid atmosphere, the accretions of

[1] Sermon 68.
[2] Cardinal Wiseman, *Fabiola*.

" The kingdom of heaven is like a net, that was cast into the sea, and enclosed fish of every kind at once " [*Matthew 13.47*]

" He brought them to the haven they wished for " [*Psalm 106.30*]

filth, the dampness, the intense cold, the tragic associations of the place, must have made confinement in it worse than death."[1]

It was the great fire that destroyed nearly half the city of Rome in A.D. 64 that roused Nero to initiate the worst persecution of Christians which had occurred until then. He accused them of being the instigators of this fire. Three or four years later—the actual date is not certain—SS. Peter and Paul were condemned to death. It was towards the end of the month of June.

Coming out from the darkness of that underground dungeon the old fisherman must have been almost blinded by the glare of the sun, for it was mid-summer. We can picture him dragging his body through the crowded streets, past the Forum and the Theatre of Marcellus, down to the banks of the Tiber. New houses are being built to replace those laid waste by the fire. The armed guards walk beside their prisoner. They cross the river, and here Peter has his last glimpse of ships and seafarers. Away to the left are the long quays where merchantmen and warships are berthed. It is fairly certain that the former fisherman must have spotted a few small fishing boats below the bridge. Did the thought occur to him at that moment that, had he not left his boat and nets to follow Jesus, he might be living in comfortable retirement beside the Sea of Galilee, instead of being dragged to crucifixion far away from his home country? Perhaps there was a man casting a line into the muddy waters of the river, where fish were abundant in those times. If so, then Peter would have remembered the day when he was bidden to cast a line into the sea, and how

[1] Chandlery, *op. cit.*, p. 179.

L

he found a silver piece in the mouth of the fish he landed. But this was long, long ago.

It was a long walk from the prison, and the sun glared down mercilessly. Eventually the soldiers and their prisoner reached the newly erected Circus of Nero, where a vast crowd had assembled, looking forward to entertainment from the sight of the last agonies of the Christians. By that date it was the most popular form of amusement in Rome. Here it was, so most archaeologists are agreed, that the fisherman-Apostle was crucified, head downwards at his own request, for he counted himself unworthy to die in the same posture as his Divine Master. After he was dead, his body was removed to a cemetery on the Appian Way. Later on it was taken back to the place of the martyrdom, and laid to rest in a tomb, above which now stands the high altar of the Vatican Basilica.

Modern pilgrims to Rome often forget that it was a busy seaport until about a hundred and fifty years ago. The district of Trastevere was the "sailor-town" of Rome in the Middle Ages. Here in 1481 Pope Sixtus IV, who was the son of a fisherman, founded a hospice for seamen. Close by was the Ripa Grande where ships of many nations were berthed. There was also a Home for English sailors, placed under the patronage of St. Edmund, king and martyr. It appears to have been closed after the Reformation, when most English seamen had become Protestants. Seafarers in the port of Rome had their own Oratory on the banks of the Tiber. It was dedicated to Our Lady of the Good Voyage.

To-day no ships find their way up the Tiber. The only vessels to be found on the brown muddy waters of the river are a few small boats and skiffs. But just on nineteen hundred years after the martyrdom of the Fisherman Pope an International Secretariate of the Apostleship of the Sea was set up in Rome, and placed under the supreme direction of the Sacred Consistorial Council, which has been entrusted with the care of all classes of displaced persons, of whom seafarers are the most numerous. It seems fitting that its offices should be located close to the Church of S. Apollinare, the Bishop of Ravenna, who was a disciple of Peter the Fisherman.

Every year, on the twenty-ninth day of June, the Responsories in the office of Matins remind us how Simon Peter was called from a ship, and made a prince over the people of God, and given the keys of the kingdom of heaven. Then, later on in the Second Nocturn of Matins, come the words:

> " Lord, if it be thou, bid me come to thee on the waters. . . ." And Jesus, stretching forth his hand, took hold of him, and said to him: " O thou of little faith, why didst thou doubt? "
>
> . . . But seeing a strong wind coming, he was afraid; and when he began to sink, he cried out saying: " Lord, save me."

On the following morning, June 30th, when the Church commemorates the martyrdom of St. Paul, the fifth antiphon at Lauds recalls how this great voyager " suffered shipwreck thrice for the name of Christ ".

Six days later—the Octave day of SS. Peter and Paul—the Collect sums up with Latin brevity and conciseness the relationship between Christ and these two seafarers:

O God, whose right hand upheld blessed Peter from sinking when he walked upon the waves, and delivered his fellow apostle from the depth of the sea, when thrice he suffered shipwreck: graciously hear ue, and grant that, through their united merits, we may obtain eternal glory.

APPENDICES

APPENDIX I

Bless and keep safe, O Jesus,
All who pass over the seas
Which thou hast wonderfully made,
From which thou didst take thy first Apostles,
Which, dwelling among us,
Thou didst tame by thy touch,
Subduing them also to thy children's purpose
By thy divising in their minds,
By thy courage in their hearts,
By thy skill in their hands.

Convert the minds and hearts of wicked men,
From making into instruments of death
Thy gifts bestowed for good and happiness.

Hear the prayers of mothers and wives and children,
Of hearts wounded by long separation and uncertainty.

Give to captains, officers and men
Skill, courage and endurance,
Thy character and virtue;
To the masters of powerful engines
Thy greater power of human brain and heart.

May we the people of the sea-ports
To which are brought by sailors every day
At the risk of their own lives
Thy children and thy gifts,
May we value our privilege to make for thy sailors
A haven from every danger to body and to soul,
Such a home as they need, and we owe.

To all sailors, O Jesus,
And to all living souls by thee entrusted to them,
Give a clear mind to steer thy course,
Wisdom and courage to hold it
Safely to thy appointed haven
Of happiness unending.   Amen.

T. D. ROBERTS, S.J.
Formerly Archbishop of Bombay

APPENDIX II

Matthew

4.18–22.   Jesus calls the four fishermen-Apostles, who were "casting a net into the sea", and "repairing their nets".

8.14.   Jesus goes to the house of Peter, the fisherman, and heals his wife's mother of a fever.

23–27.   He takes ship, and checks the winds and the sea.

9.1.   He takes ship across the sea to "his own city".

11.20–24.   He curses the fishing towns of Bethsaida, Capharnaum and Corozain.

13.47–49.   The parable of the net cast into the sea.

14.13.   Jesus takes ship to withdraw into desert country, where he disembarks.

17.   He feeds the five thousand with two fishes and five loaves, orders the disciples to take ship.

22–33.   He appears to them, walking on the sea during a storm.

15.34.   He feeds the four thousand with a "few small fishes" and seven loaves.

39.   He goes on board the ship and crosses to the region of Magedan.

16.5.   Jesus and his Apostles cross the sea, and find they have no bread with them.

17.26.   Peter casts his hook and finds a silver coin in the fish's mouth.

Mark

1.16–21.   Jesus calls the four fishermen-Apostles.

29.   He goes with them to the house of Andrew and Simon, and cures their mother of a fever.

2.13.   He teaches by the sea.

Mark

4.1.   He again teaches by the sea, and then goes aboard a boat, to be heard better.

35–40.   He crosses the sea, and checks the wind and the waves during a storm.

5.1.   Having landed in the centre of the Gerasenes (21), he " went back by boat across the sea ".

6.32.   Jesus and the Apostles take ship and make for " a lonely place ".

34–44.   He feeds five thousand with two fishes and five loaves.

45.   He prevails on the disciples to take ship and cross to Bethsaida.

47–53.   During a storm they behold him walking on the sea; land at Genesareth, and moor the boat there.

8.7–9.   He feeds four thousand with " a few small fishes " and seven loaves.

10.   Having embarked for Dalmanutha, the Apostles find they have " no more than one loaf in the boat " (v. 15).

9.32.   Jesus and the Apostles go to the house of Peter at Capharnaum, where he bids them become as little children.

49.   He tells them they must " have salt " in themselves.

Luke

4.38.   Jesus goes to the house of Simon, the fisherman, and heals his mother-in-law of a violent fever.

5.1–11.   He preaches from Peter's boat; bids the fishermen let down their nets, and both boats are filled with fish. The fishermen are called to be " fishers of men ".

6.17.   He does down to " the sea-coast of Tyre and Sidon ".

Luke

8.22–25. The disciples embark in a boat. Jesus falls asleep, and calms the storm at sea.

27. They go ashore in the country of the Gerasenes.

9.13–17. Jesus feeds five thousand with two fishes and five loaves.

10.13–16. He curses the fisher towns of Corozain, Bethsaida and Capharnaum.

John

1.35–44. Jesus calls the first four fishermen-Apostles.

6.1. He " retires across the sea of Galilee ".

9–14. He feeds the five thousand with five barley loaves and two fishes.

15–21. The disciples embark in their boat. Jesus walks on the sea, and comes on board.

21.1–14. He appears to the fishermen on the shore, and they catch many fish.

APPENDIX III

Events	Matthew	Mark	Luke	John
Call of the four fishermen-Apostles	4.18–22	1.16–21		1.37–51
Jesus preaches on the sea-shore at Capharnaum	4.13–17		4.31	
Final call of the four fishermen-Apostles	4.18–22	1.16–20	5.1–11	
Jesus heals Peter's mother-in-law	8.14–15	1.30–32	4.38–39	
He takes ship across the sea	9.1			6.1
Parable of the net	13.47			
Jesus calms the storm at sea	8.24–27	4.37–40	8.23 25	
Feeding of the five thousand	14.13–21	6.30–44	9.12–17	6.1–13
Jesus walks upon the sea	14.22–33	6.45–54		6.15–21
Feeding of the four thousand	15.32–39	8.1–9		
Jesus visits the sea-coast of Tyre and Sidon	15.21	7.24		
Jesus and the Apostles cross the sea. St. Peter's confession of Christ	16.13–21	8.27–30		

Events	Matthew	Mark	Luke	John
Three of the four fishermen are witnesses of the Transfiguration	17.1–8	9.1–7	9.28–36	
The coin found in the fish's mouth	17.26			
Jesus refers to salt		9.49		
Anger of the two " Sons of Thunder "			9.54–56	
Jesus curses the fisher towns of Galilee	11.20–24		10.13–16	
The mother of James and John asks for special honours for her fishermen sons	20.20–28	10.35–45		
Jesus washes Peter's feet				13.1–17
Peter warned	26.34	14.30	22.34	13.38
The fishermen-Apostles sleep in Gethsemani	26.40–45	14.37–41	22.43–46	
Peter smites Malchus	26.51	14.47	22.50	18.10
Peter follows Christ	26.58	14.54	22.55	18.15
Peter denies Christ	26.69–75	14.66–72	22.54–62	18.17–27
Peter and John run to the tomb			24.12	20.3
Christ appears to Peter			24.34	

Events	Matthew	Mark	Luke	John
And to the Apostles by the Sea of Galilee				21.1–24
Jesus bids Peter "Feed my sheep"				21.15–17

APPENDIX IV

(A) CONCORDANCE OF THE CHIEF MARITIME WORDS USED IN THE NEW TESTAMENT (DOUAY VERSION)[1]

ANCHOR

Acts

27.29   they cast four anchors out of the stern

40   when they had taken up the anchors

Hebrews

6.19   which we have as an anchor of the soul, sure and firm

BOAT

Matthew

8.23   entered into a boat, his disciples . . .

24   the boat was covered with waves

9.1   entering into a boat, came into his own city

13.2   he went up into a boat, and sat . . .

14.13   he retired from thence by a boat into a desert place

22   obliged his disciples to go into the boat

24   but the boat in the midst of the sea was tossed with the waves

29   Peter going down out of the boat, walked . . .

32   came up into the boat, the wind ceased

33   and they that were in the boat came and adored him

Acts

27.16   we had much work to come by the boat

30   having let down the boat into the sea

32   the soldiers cut off the ropes of the boat

FISH

Matthew

7.10   if he shall ask him a fish, will he reach him a serpent?

17.26   that fish which shall first come up, take

[1] The wording of the Authorized Version is generally the same in the New Testament.

Luke

11.11   Or a fish, will he for a fish give him a serpent?

24.42   they offered him a piece of broiled fish

John

21.9   they saw hot coals lying, and a fish laid thereon

13   Jesus cometh and taketh . . . fish in like manner

Fishes

Matthew

13.47   The kingdom of heaven is like to . . . all kinds of fishes

14.17   We have not here but . . . two fishes

15.34   But they said: Seven, and a few little fishes

36   and taking . . . the fishes and giving thanks

Mark

6.38   they say, five, and two fishes

41   And when . . . the two fishes

41   the two fishes he divided among them all

43   they took up the leavings . . . and of the fishes

8.7   and they had a few little fishes

Luke

5.6   they enclosed a very great multitude of fishes

9   he was wholly astonished . . . at the draught of fishes

9.13   we have . . . five loaves and two fishes

9.16   And taking . . . and the two fishes

John

6.9   there is a boy here that hath five barley loaves and two fishes

11   Jesus distributed . . . in like manner also of the fishes

21.6   they were not able to draw it, for the multitude of fishes

8   the other disciples . . . dragging the net with fishes

10   bring hither of the fishes which you have now caught

11   Simon Peter . . . drew the net to land . . . full of great fishes

I Corinthians

15.39   all flesh is not the same flesh but . . . another of fishes

FISHERMEN

Mark

1.16   Simon and Andrew . . . casting nets into the sea (for they were fishermen)

Luke

5.2   but the fishermen were gone out of them, and were washing their nets

FISHERS

Matthew

4.18   . . . casting a net into the sea (for they were fishers)

19   I will make you to be fishers of men

Mark

1.17   I will make you to become fishers of men

FISHING

John

21.3   Simon Peter saith . . . I go a fishing

MIDST OF THE SEA

Matthew

14.24   But the boat was in the midst of the sea

Mark

6.47   the ship was in the midst of the sea

ROWED

John

6.19   when they had rowed . . . about five and twenty or thirty furlongs

ROWING

Mark

6.48   seeing them labouring in rowing

RUDDER

Acts

27.40   loosing withal the rudder bands

SAIL

Acts

20.3   the Jews laid wait for him, as he was about to sail
  16   Paul had determined to sail by Ephesus
21.1   we set sail, and came . . . to Coos
27.1   it was determined that he should sail into Italy
   2   we launched, meaning to sail by the coasts of Asia
  12   the greatest part gave counsel to sail thence
  17   they let down the sail yard, and so were driven
  24   God hath given thee all them that sail with thee
28.10 when we were to set sail, they laded us with such
       things as were necessary

Apocalypse

18.17 all that sail into the lake and mariners, as many
       as work in the sea, stood afar off

SAILED

Luke

8.26   they sailed to the country of the Gerasens

Acts

13.4   from thence they sailed to Cyprus
  13   they sailed from Paphos, and came to Perge
14.25 they sailed to Antioch, from whence they had
       been delivered
15.39 taking Mark, sailed to Cyprus
18.18 Paul . . . taking his leave of the brethren, sailed
       thence into Syria
20.6   we sailed from Philippi
  13   going aboard the ship, sailed to Assos
21.3   we sailed into Syria, and came to Tyre
27.4   we sailed under Cyprus
   7   for many days we had sailed slowly: we sailed
       near Crete by Salmone
  13   they sailed close by Crete
28.11 after three months we sailed in a ship of
       Alexandria

SAILING

Luke

8.23   when they were sailing, he slept

M

Acts

16.11   sailing from Troas, we came with a straight
        course to Samothracia

20.15   sailing thence . . . we came over against Chios

21.2   when we had found a ship sailing over to Phenice
        . . . and set forth

27.5   sailing over the sea of Cilicia . . . we came to
        Lystra

6   a ship of Alexandria, sailing into Italy

8   with much ado sailing by it . . . we came into
        . . . Goodhavens

9   when sailing now was dangerous . . . Paul
        comforted them

27   as we were sailing in Adria . . . the shipmen
        deemed they had discovered some country

SEA

Matthew

4.15   way of the sea beyond Jordan

18   his brother, casting a net into the sea

8.24   great tempest arose in the sea

36   he commanded the winds and the sea

27   the winds and the sea obey him (Mark 4.40)

32   down a steep place into the sea

13.47   like a net cast into the sea

14.25   to them walking on the sea

26   seeing him walking on the sea

17.26   go to the sea, and cast in a hook

18.6   be crowned in the depth of the sea

21.21   cast thyself into the sea

23.15   you go round about the sea

Mark

1.16   And passing by the sea of Galilee . . . casting
        their nets into the sea, for they . . .

3.7   retired with his disciples to the sea

4.1   went into a ship, and sat in the sea

39   rebuked the wind, and said to the sea

5.1   they came over the strait of the sea

13   was carried headlong into the sea

13.15   were stifled in the sea

Mark

13.21   he was nigh unto the sea, and there
9.41   his neck, and he were cast into the sea
11.23   thou removed and be cast into the sea

Luke

8.25   commandeth both the winds and the sea
17.2   his neck, and be cast into the sea
6   be thou transplanted into the sea
21.25   roaring of the sea and of the waves

John

6.16   his disciples went down to the sea
17   they went over the sea to Capharnaum
18   the sea arose by reason of a great wind
22   the multitudes stood on the other side of the sea
25   they found him on the other side of the sea
21.1   shewed himself again to the disciples at the sea of Tiberias
7   Peter . . . cast himself into the sea

Acts

4.24   that didst make the sea, and all things . . .
14.14   who made . . . the sea and all things
17.14   sent away Paul, to go unto the sea
21.7   we, having finished the voyage by sea
27.5   and sailing over the sea of Cilicia
38   ship, casting wheat into the sea
40   they committed themselves to the sea where the seas met . . .
41   part was broken with the violence of the sea
43   cast themselves first into the sea
28.4   who, though he had escaped the sea
27.30   having let down the boat into the sea

I Corinthians

10.1   the cloud, and all passed through the sea

II Corinthians

11.25   a night and a day I was in the depth of the sea
26   in perils in the sea, in perils from . . .

James

1.6   is like a wave of the sea, which . . .

Jude
13   raging waves of the sea, foaming out

Apocalypse
4.6   sea of glass like to crystal
5.13   such as are in the sea
7.1   blow upon the earth, not upon the sea
2   given to hurt the earth and the sea
3   hurt not the earth, nor the sea
8.8   mountain . . . was cast into the sea
8   the third part of the sea became blood
9   creatures died which had life in the sea
10.2   set his right foot upon the sea
5   standing upon the sea, and upon . . .
6   the sea and the things which are therein
8   who standeth upon the sea, and upon
13.1   I saw a beast coming up out of the sea
14.7   that made heaven and earth, the sea . . .
15.2   I saw as it were a sea of glass
2   . . . standing on the sea of glass
16.3   the second angel poured out his vial upon the sea
3   . . . and every living soul died in the sea
18.17   as many as work in the sea, stood afar off
19   all were made rich, that had ships at sea
21   took up . . . a great millstone, and cast it into
the sea
20.13   the sea gave up the dead that were in it
21   and the sea is now no more

SEA COAST

Matthew
4.13   dwelt in Capharnaum on the sea coast

Luke
6.17   the sea coast both of Tyre and Sidon

SHIP

Matthew
4.21   in a ship, with Zebedee their father

Mark
1.19   were mending their nets in the ship
20   their father Zebedee in the ship

Mark

3.9   that a small ship should wait on him, because of the multitudes

4.1   he went up into a ship and sat in the sea

36   they take him even as he was in the ship

37   the waves beat into the ship, so that the ship was filled

38   and he was in the hinder part of the ship

5.2   and as he went out of the ship, immediately there met him

18   and when he went up into the ship, he that had been troubled with the devil . . .

21   when Jesus had passed again in the ship over the strait

6.32   going into a ship, they went into a desert place apart

45   immediately he obliged his disciples to go up into the ship

47   when it was late, the ship was in the midst of the sea

51   he went up to them into the ship, and the wind ceased

8.10   immediately going up into a ship with his disciples

13   he went up again into the ship and passed to the other side of the water

14   they had but one loaf with them in the ship

Luke

3   going in to one of the ships . . . he taught the multitudes out of the ship

8.22   he went up into a little ship with his disciples

37   he going up into the ship, returned back again

John

6.17   when they had gone up into a ship, they went over the sea to Capharnaum

19   they see Jesus . . . drawing nigh to the ship

21   they were willing therefore to take him into the ship

21   and presently the ship was at the land to which they were going

John

6.22	the multitude . . . saw that there was no other ship but one
22	and that Jesus had not entered into the ship with his disciples
21.3	they went forth and entered into the ship
6	Cast the net on the right side of the ship
8	the other disciples came in the ship

Acts

20.13	but we, going aboard the ship, sailed to Assos
38	and they brought him on his way to the ship
21.2	when we had found a ship sailing over to Phenice, we went aboard
3	came to Tyre, for there the ship was to unlade her burden
6	when we had bid one another farewell, we took ship
27.2	going on board a ship of Adrumetum, we launched
6	the centurion, finding a ship of Alexandria, sailing into Italy
10	with injury . . . not only of the lading and ship, but also of our lives
11	the centurion believed the pilot and the master of the ship more than . . . Paul
15	when the ship was caught and could not bear up against the wind
17	they used helps, undergirding the ship
18	the next day they lightened the ship
19	they cast out with their own hands the tackling of the ship
22	no loss of any man's life . . . but only of the ship
30	they would have cast anchors out of the forepart of the ship
30	the shipmen sought to fly out of the ship
31	except these stay in the ship, you cannot be saved
37	we were in all in the ship two hundred three-score and sixteen souls
38	they lightened the ship, casting the wheat into the sea

Acts

27.39   they minded, if they could, to thrust in the ship

41   where two seas met, they run the ship aground

44   some they carried . . . on those things that belonged to the ship

28.11   we sailed in a ship of Alexandria that had wintered in the island

SHIPS

Mark

4.36   there were other ships with him

Luke

5.2   and saw two ships standing by the lake

3   going into one of the ships that was Simon's

7   they came and filled both ships

11   having brought their ships to land . . . they followed him

John

6.23   other ships came in from Tiberias

James

3.4   behold also ships . . . driven by strong winds

Apocalypse

8.9   the third part of the ships was destroyed

18.19   that great city . . . that had ships at sea . . . is made desolate

SHIPWRECK

II Corinthians

11.25   thrice I suffered shipwreck

I Timothy

1.19   a good conscience, which some rejected have made shipwreck concerning the faith

WATER (SEA)

Matthew

8.18   gave orders to pass over the water

28   when he was come on the other side of the water into the country of the Gerasenes

9.1   he passed over the water and came into his own city

Matthew

14.22   Jesus obliged his disciples . . . to go before him over the water

29   Peter . . . walked upon the water to come to Jesus

16.5   when his disciples were come over the water, they had forgotten to take bread

Mark

4.45   he obliged his disciples . . . that they might go before him over the water

8.13   leaving them . . . he passed to the other side of the water

Luke

8.24   he rebuked . . . the rage of the water

WATERS

Matthew

14.28   bid me come to thee upon the waters

II Corinthians

11.28   in perils of waters

Apocalypse

14.2   as the noise of many waters

19.6   as the voice of many waters . . . saying Alleluia

WAVES

Matthew

8.24   so that the boat was covered with waves

14.24   the boat was tossed with the waves

Mark

4.37   the waves beat into the ship

Luke

21.25   . . . distress of nations, by reason of the confusion of the roaring of the sea and of the waves

Jude

13   raging waves of the sea, foaming out their own confusion

(B) CONCORDANCE OF THE CHIEF MARITIME WORDS FOUND IN THE OLD TESTAMENT (DOUAY AND AUTHORIZED VERSIONS)

As it may be presumed that the fishermen-Apostles would be specially familiar with the passages in the Old Testament dealing with the sea, ships, and fishes, etc., this maritime concordance is included.

FISH

Numbers
11.5   we remember the fish we ate

II Paralipomenon (A.V. *II Chronicles*)
33.14   from the entering in of the fish gate

II Esdras (A.V. *Nehemiah*)
3.3   the fish gate the sons of Asnaa built
13.16   brought fish and all manner of wares

Tobias (A.V. *Tobit*)
6.2   a monstrous fish came up to devour him, etc.

Jonas (A.V. *Jonah*)
2.1   the Lord prepared a great fish, etc.

Sophonias (A.V. *Zephaniah*)
1.10   the noise of a cry from the fish gate

FISHERS

Isaias (A.V. *Isaiah*)
19.18   the fishers shall mourn

Jeremias (A.V. *Jeremiah*)
16.16   I will send many fishers

Ezechiel (A.V. *Ezekiel*)
47.10   the fishers shall stand over these waters

FISHES

Genesis
1.26   let him have dominion over the fishes of the sea
28   Rule over the fishes of the sea
9.2   all the fishes of the sea are delivered into your hand

N

Numbers

11.22 shall the fishes of the sea be gathered together . . . ?

Deuteronomy

4.18 lest . . . you might make you a graven simili-
tude . . . of fishes that abide in the waters
under the earth

III Kings (A.V. *I Kings*)

4.33 he discoursed . . . of creeping things, and of
fishes

Job

12.8 the fishes of the sea shall tell

40.26 wilt thou fill . . . the cabins of fishes with his
head?

Ecclesiastes

9.12 as fishes are taken with the hook . . . so men
are taken

Psalms

8.9 the fishes of the sea that pass through the paths
of the sea

Isaias (A.V. *Isaiah*)

50.2 the fishes shall rot for want of water and shall die
for thirst

Ezechiel (A.V. *Ezekiel*)

38.20 so that the fishes of the sea . . . shall be moved
at my presence

47.9 there shall be fishes in abundance

10 many sorts of the fishes thereof, as the fishes of
the great sea, a very great multitude

Osee (A.V. *Hosea*)

4.3 yea, the fishes of the sea also shall be gathered
together

Habacuc (A.V. *Habakkuk*)

1.13 thou wilt make men as the fishes of the sea

Sophonias (A.V. *Zephaniah*)

1.3 I will gather . . . the fishes of the sea

GREAT SEA

Psalms

103.25 (A.V. 104.25)
    so is this great sea, which stretcheth wide its arms

Ezechiel (A.V. *Ezekiel*)

47.10 as the fishes of the great sea

   15 from the great sea by way of Hethalon

   19 and the torrent even to the great sea

48.28 the inheritance over against the great sea

Daniel

7.2 the winds strove upon the great sea

HAVEN

Psalms

106.30 (A.V. 107.30)
    he brought them to the haven which they wished for

I Machabees

14.5 he took Joppe for a haven

II Machabees

14.1 by the haven of Tripolis to place

HOOK

Isaias (A.V. *Isaiah*)

19.8 All that cast a hook . . .

MIDST OF THE SEA

Proverbs

23.34 thou shalt be as one sleeping in the midst of the sea, and as a pilot fast asleep, when the stern is lost

30.19 I am utterly ignorant of . . . the way of a ship in the midst of the sea

Ezechiel (A.V. *Ezekiel*)

26.5 she shall be a drying place for nets in the midst of the sea

27.32 what city is like Tyre, which is become silent in the midst of the sea?

NETS (FISHING)

Isaias (A.V. *Isaiah*)
   19.8   they that spread nets upon the waters shall languish away

Ezechiel (A.V. *Ezekiel*)
   26.5   she shall be a drying place for nets in the midst of the sea
   47.10   from Engaddi even to Engallim there shall be drying of nets

SAIL

III Kings (A.V. *I Kings*)
   22.49   to sail into Ophir for gold

Ecclesiasticus
   43.26   let them that sail on the sea

Isaias (A.V. *Isaiah*)
   23.12   arise and sail over to Cethim

Ezechiel (A.V. *Ezekiel*)
   27.7   linen from Egypt was woven for thy sail

SAILED

I Machabees
   13.29   by all that sailed on the sea

SAILORS

III Kings (A.V. *I Kings*)
   9.27   sailors that had knowledge of the sea

SEA

Genesis
   1.10   God, gathering together of the waters, he called Seas
     22   increase and multiply, and fill the waters of the sea
   9.2   all the fishes of the sea are delivered into your hand
   14.3   . . . into the woodland vale, which is now the salt sea

Exodus

14.2   you shall encamp before it upon the sea

16   stretch forth thy hand over the sea, and divide it

21   when Moses had stretched forth his hand over the sea

22   the children of Israel went in through the midst of the sea dried up

23   the Egyptian pursuing went in after them . . . through the midst of the sea

27   when Moses had stretched forth his hand towards the sea

29   the children of Israel marched through the midst of the sea

31   and they saw the Egyptians dead upon the sea shore

15.1   the horse and the rider he hath thrown into the sea

4   Pharaoh's chariots and his army he hath cast into the sea . . . his chosen captains are drowned in the Red Sea

10   The wind blew and the sea covered them

19   Pharaoh went in on horseback . . . into the sea . . . the Lord brought back upon them the waters of the sea

21   Let us sing to the Lord, the horse and his rider he hath thrown into the sea

22   Moses brought Israel from the Red Sea

20.11   In six days the Lord made heaven and earth, and the sea

23.31   I will set thy bounds from the Red Sea to the sea of the Philistines

Leviticus

11.9   all that hath fins and scales, as well in the sea . . . you shall eat

Numbers

11.22   shall the fishes of the sea be gathered together to fill them?

31   a wind going out from the Lord, taking quails beyond the sea

13.30   the Chanaanite abideth by the sea

Numbers

34.5   the limits . . . shall end in the shore of the great sea

11   thence they shall come eastward to the sea of Genereth

Deuteronomy

11.24   unto the western sea shall be your borders

30.13   nor is it beyond the sea . . . which of us can cross the sea?

33.19   who shall suck as milk the abundance of the sea?

23   he shall possess the sea and the south

34.2   the Lord showed him . . . all the land of Juda unto the furthermost sea

Josue (A.V. *Joshua*)

15.4   the bounds thereof shall be the great sea

47   even to the great sea that is the border thereof

16.6   the confines go out unto the sea

19.29   the outgoings thereof shall be at the sea

III Kings (A.V. *I Kings*)

5, 8, 9   cedar trees . . . from Libanus to the sea, and I will put them together in floats in the sea

9.27   Hiram sent his servants in the fleet, sailors that had knowledge of the sea

10.22   the king's navy, once in three years, went . . . by sea to Tharsis

18.43   he said to his servant: Go up, and look toward the sea

44   a little cloud arose out of the sea, like a man's foot

22.49   Josaphat made navies on the sea to sail into Ophir

I Paralipomenon (A.V. *I Chronicles*)

16.32   let the sea roar and the fulness thereof

II Paralipomenon (A.V. *II Chronicles*)

2.16   we will cut down trees out of Libanus . . . and will convey them in floats by sea to Joppe

Tobias (A.V. *Tobit*)

8.7   Lord God of our fathers, may . . . the sea . . . bless thee

Judith

2.14   he forced all the stately cities there . . . till one comes to the sea

5.12   the God of heaven opened the sea to them in their flight . . . they walked through the bottom of the sea

Job

9.8   he walketh upon the waves of the sea

11.9   the measure of him . . . is broader than the sea

12.8   speak to the earth . . . and the fishes of the sea shall tell

14.11   as if the waters should depart out of the sea

28.14   and the sea saith, it is not with me

36.30   he shall cover also the ends of the sea

38.8   who shut up the sea with doors, when it broke forth . . .

16   Hast thou entered into the depths of the sea?

41.22   he shall make the deep sea to boil like a pot, and shall make it as when ointments boil

Psalms

8.9   the fishes of the sea that pass through the paths of the sea

32.7 (A.V. 33.7, 3)
   gathering together the waters of the sea, as in a vessel

45.3 (A.V. 46.2, 1)
   the mountains shall be removed into the heart of the sea

64.8 (A.V. 65.7)
   Thou, who troublest the depths of the sea, the noise of its waves

65.6 (A.V. 66.6)
   who turneth the sea into dry land

67.22 (A.V. 68.22)
   the Lord said: I will turn them into the depth of the sea

68.3 (A.V. 68.3)
   I am come into the depth of the sea; and a tempest hath overwhelmed me

Psalms

68.35 (A.V. 69.34)
>> let the heavens . . . praise him: the sea, and
>> everything that creepeth therein

71.8 (A.V. 72.8)
>> he shall rule from sea to sea

76.20 (A.V. 77.19)
>> thy way is in the sea, and thy paths in many
>> waters

77.53 (A.V. 78.53)
>> and the sea overwhelmed their enemies

79.12 (A.V. 80.11)
>> it stretched forth its branches unto the sea

88.10 (A.V. 89.9)
>> thou rulest the power of the sea: and appeasest
>> the motion of the waves thereof

88.13 the north and the sea thou hath created [the
>> sea is *south* in A.V. 89.12]

   26 (A.V. 89.25)
>> I will set his hand in the sea

92.4 (A.V. 93.4)
>> wonderful are the surges of the sea

94.5 (A.V. 95.5)
>> for the sea is his and he made it

95.11 (A.V. 96.11)
>> let the sea be moved, and the fulness thereof

105.7 (A.V. 106.7)
>> they provoked to wrath going up to the sea, even
>> the Red Sea

106.3 (A.V. nil)
>> from the rising of the sun . . . and from the sea

   23 (A.V. 107.23)
>> they that go down to the sea in ships, doing
>> business in great waters

113.3 (A.V. 114.3)
>> the sea saw and fled

   5 (A.V. 114.5)
>> what ailed thee, O thou sea, that thou didst flee?

134.6 (A.V. 135.6)
>> whatsoever the Lord pleased he hath done . . .
>> in the sea, and in all the deeps

Psalms

138.9 (A.V. 139.9)
> if I take my wings early in the morning, and dwell in the uttermost parts of the sea

145.6 (A.V. 146.6)
> whose hope is in the Lord his God, who made . . . the sea

Proverbs

8.29
> when he compassed the sea with its bounds . . . I was with him forming all things

Ecclesiastes

1.7
> all the rivers run into the sea, yet the sea doth not overflow

Wisdom

5.23   the water of the sea shall rage against them

10.19   their enemies she drowned in the sea

14.3   for thou hast made a way even in the sea, and a most sure path among the waves

4   shewing that thou art able to save out of all things, yea though a man went to sea without art

5   therefore men also trust their lives even to a little wood, and passing over the sea by ship are saved

19.12   the quail came up to them from the sea

Ecclesiasticus

18.8   as a drop of water of the sea are they esteemed

24.8   I alone have . . . walked in the waves of the sea

39   for her thoughts are more vast than the sea: and her counsels more deep than the great ocean

29.23   evil surety ship . . . hath tossed them as a wave of the sea

40.11   all waters shall return to the sea

43.26   let them that sail on the sea tell the dangers thereof: and when we hear with our ears we shall admire

44.23   that he would exalt his seed as the stars, and they should inherit from sea to sea

50.3   in his days the wells . . . flowed out, and were filled as the sea above measure

Isaias (A.V. *Isaiah*)

5.30	they shall make a noise . . . like the roaring of the sea
9.1	the way of the sea beyond Jordan . . . was heavily loaded
10.26	the Lord of hosts shall lift his rod over the sea
11.9	the earth is filled with the knowledge of the Lord, as the covering waters of the sea
11	the Lord shall set his hand . . . from the islands of the sea
16.8	they are gone over the sea
17.12	woe to the multitude of many people, like the multitude of the roaring sea
18.2	woe to the land . . . that sendeth ambassadors by sea
19.5	the water of the sea shall be dried up
21.1	the burden of the desert of the sea
23.1	howl, ye ships of the sea
2	the merchants of Sidon, passing over the seas have filled thee
4	be thou ashamed, O Sidon, for the sea speaketh, even the strength of the sea
11	he stretched out his hand over the sea
24.14	they shall make a joyful noise from the sea
15	glorify ye the Lord . . . is the islands of the sea
27.1	the Lord shall slay the whale that is in the sea
42.10	sing ye to the Lord . . . you that go down to the sea
43.16	who made a way in the sea, and a path in the mighty waters
48.18	that thy justice had been as the waves of the sea
50.2	at my rebuke I will make the sea a desert
51.10	hast not thou dried up the sea? . . . who madest the depth of the sea away
15	I am the Lord thy God, who trouble the sea, and the waves thereof swell
57.20	the wicked are like the raging sea which cannot rest
60.5	thy heart shall wonder . . . when the multitude of the sea shall be converted to thee

Isaias (A.V. *Isaiah*)

60.9 for the islands wait for me, and the ships of the sea in the beginning; that I may bring thy sons from afar

63.11 where is he that brought them up out of the sea?

66.19 I will set a sign . . . to the Gentiles into the sea

Jeremias (A.V. *Jeremiah*)

5.22 I have set the sand a bound for the sea

6.23 their voice shall roar, like the sea

25.22 the kings of the land of the islands that are beyond the sea

31.35 thus saith the Lord . . . who stirreth up the sea, and the waves thereof roar

48.32 they are come even to the sea of Jaser: thy branches are gone over the sea

49.23 they are troubled as in the sea

50.42 their voice shall roar like the sea

51.36 I will make her sea desolate

42 the sea is come up over Babylon: she is covered with the multitude of the waves thereof

Lamentations

2.13 for great as the sea is thy destruction

4.3 even the sea monsters have drawn out thy breast

Baruch

3.30 who hath passed over the sea and found her?

Ezechiel (A.V. *Ezekiel*)

1.16 four living creatures . . . the work of them was like the appearance of the sea

26.3 I will cause many nations to come up to thee, as the waves of the sea rise up

16 all the princes of the sea shall come down from off their thrones

17 how art thou fallen, that dwellest in the sea, renowned city that wast strong in the sea

18 the islands in the sea shall be troubled

27.3 say to Tyre that dwelleth at the entry of the sea

4 I am of perfect beauty, and situate in the heart of the sea

5 they have built thee, with all sea planks

Ezechiel (A.V. *Ezekiel*)

27.9   all the ships of the sea and their mariners were thy factors

25   the ships of the sea were thy chief in thy merchandise . . . thou wast glorified exceedingly in the heart of the sea

26   the south wind hath broken thee in the heart of the sea

27   the multitude that is in the midst of thee shall fall into the heart of the sea

29   the mariners and all the pilots of the sea shall stand upon the land

33   thy merchandise that went from thee by sea didst fill many people

34   now thou art destroyed by the sea

28.2   I sit in the chair of God in the heart of the sea

8   thou shalt die the death of them that are slain in the heart of the sea

32.2   thou art like the dragon that is in the sea

38.20   the fishes of the sea . . . shall be moved at my presence

47.8   these waters . . . shall go into the sea

Daniel

7.3   four beasts came up out of the sea

Osee (A.V. *Hosea*)

4.3   the fishes of the sea also shall be gathered together

11.10   the children of the sea shall fear

Joel

2.20   I will drive . . . with his face towards the east sea, and his hinder part towards the utmost sea

Amos

5.8   Seek him . . . that calleth the waters of the sea

8.12   they shall move from sea to sea

9.3   though they hide themselves from my eyes in the depth of the sea

6   he who calleth the waters of the sea

Jonas (A.V. *Jonah*)

1.4 the Lord sent a great wind into the sea; and a great tempest was raised in the sea

5 they cast forth the wares . . . into the sea

9 I fear the Lord the God of heaven who made both the sea and the dry land

11 what shall we do to thee, that the sea may be calm to us? For the sea flowed and swelled

12 take me up and cast me into the sea, and the sea shall be calm to you

13 the sea tossed and swelled upon them

15 they took Jonas and cast him into the sea: and the sea ceased from raging

2.4 thou hast cast me forth into the deep in the heart of the sea

6 the sea hath covered my head

Micheas (A.V. *Micah*)

7.12 in that day they shall come . . . from sea to sea

19 he will cast all our sins into the bottom of the sea

Nahum

1.4 he rebuketh the sea and drieth it up

3.8 the sea is its riches; the waters are its walls

Habacuc (A.V. *Habakkuk*)

1.14 thou wilt make men as the fishes of the sea

2.14 that men may know the glory of the Lord, as waters covering the sea

3.8 Wast thy indignation in the sea?

15 thou madest a way in the sea for thy horses

Sophonias (A.V. *Zephaniah*)

1.3 I will gather . . . the fishes of the sea

Aggeus (A.V. *Haggai*)

2.7 Yet a little while, and I will move . . . the sea

Zacharias (A.V. *Zechariah*)

9.4 the Lord shall strike her strength in the sea

10 his power shall be from sea to sea

10.11 he shall pass over the strait of the sea and shall strike the waves in the sea

14.8 half of them to the east sea, and half of them to the last sea

I Machabees

4.23	purple of the sea and great riches
6.29	from the islands of the sea, hired troops
8.23	good success be to . . . the people of the Jews, by sea
32	we will make war against thee by sea
13.29	the arms ships carved, which might be seen by all that sailed on the sea
14.5	he made an entrance to the isles of the sea
34	he fortified Joppe, which lieth by the sea
15.1	King Antiochus sent letters from the isles of the sea
14	and the ships drew near by sea

II Machabees

5.21	that he might now make . . . the sea passable on foot
9.8	he that seemed to himself to command even the waves of the sea

SHIP

Proverbs

31.14	she is like the merchant's ship; she bringeth her bread from afar

Wisdom

5.10	as a ship that passeth through the waves, whereof when it is gone by, the trace cannot be found, nor the path of its keel in the waters

Ecclesiasticus

33.2	dashed in pieces as a ship in a storm

Isaias (A.V. *Isaiah*)

30.17	till you be left as the mast of a ship on the top of a mountain
33.21	no ship with oars shall pass by it, neither shall the great galleys pass through

Jonas (A.V. *Jonah*)

1.3	found a ship going to Tharsis
4	the ship was in danger to be broken
5	forth the wares that were in the ship . . . down into the inner part of the ship

I Machabees
15.37   Tryphon fled away by ship to Orthosias

SHIPS

Genesis
49.13   in the road of the ships, reaching as far as Sidon

Deuteronomy
28.68   the Lord shall bring thee again with ships into Egypt

Judges
5.17   Dan applied himself to ships

III Kings (A.V. *I Kings*)
22.49   the ships were broken in Asiongaber
50   go with thy servants in the ships

II Paralipomenon (A.V. *II Chronicles*)
8.18   Hiram sent him ships by the hands of his servants, skilful mariners
9.21   the king's ships went to Tharsis
20.36   was partner with him in making ships . . . they made the ships in Asiongaber
37   the ships are broken, and they could not go to Tharsis

Job
9.26   they have passed by as ships carrying fruits

Psalms
47.8 (A.V. 48.7)
   shall break in pieces the ships of Tharsis
103.26 (A.V. 104.20)
   there the ships shall go
106.23 (A.V. 109.23)
   they that go down to the sea in ships

Isaias (A.V. *Isaiah*)
2.16   upon all the ships of Tharsis . . . the loftiness of men shall be bowed down
23.1   howl, ye ships of the sea
43.14   the Chaldeans glorying in their ships
60.9   the ships of the sea in the beginning . . . wait for me

Ezechiel (A.V. *Ezekiel*)

26.18   now shall the ships be astonished

27.9   all the ships of the sea and their mariners were thy factors

25   the ships of the sea were the chief in thy merchandise

29   all that handled the oar shall come down from their ships

30.9   messengers in ships to destroy the confidence of Ethiopia

I Machabees

1.18   he entered into Egypt . . . with a great number of ships

8.26   neither shall they give them . . . ships

11.1   the king of Egypt gathered together . . . many ships

13.29   by the arms ships carved

15.3   I have built ships of war

II Machabees

12.9   set the haven on fire with the ships